So Clear
in My Mind

So Clear in My Mind

Alan Counsell

Hutchinson
London Melbourne Sydney Auckland Johannesburg

Hutchinson & Co. (Publishers) Ltd

An imprint of the Hutchinson Publishing Group

17–21 Conway Street, London W1P 6JD

Hutchinson Group (Australia) Pty Ltd
30–32 Cremorne Street, Richmond South, Victoria 3121
PO Box 151, Broadway, New South Wales 2007

Hutchinson Group (NZ) Ltd
32–34 View Road, PO Box 40-086, Glenfield, Auckland 10

Hutchinson Group (SA) Pty Ltd
PO Box 337, Bergvlei 2012, South Africa

First published 1982
© Alan Counsell 1982

Set in Linotron Times by Computape (Pickering) Ltd,
Pickering, North Yorkshire

Printed in Great Britain by The Anchor Press Ltd
and bound by Wm Brendon & Son Ltd,
both of Tiptree, Essex

British Library Cataloguing in Publication Data
Counsell, Alan
    So clear in my mind.
    1. Counsell, Alan   2. Spasticity – English – Biography
    I. Title
    362.4'1'0924   RC385

ISBN 0 09 149690 X

The publisher is grateful to the Lewis Textile Museum, Blackburn and Rudeni
Photography for permission to use the photograph of Audley Hall Mill.

Illustrations

Alan's mother and father in 1928
Alan at the age of three
Aunty Elsie
Mammy and Papa Earnshaw in 1950
Alan's mother and father in 1952
Mother, Alan, Tom and nephew Jim at Blackpool in 1955
Alan in 1954
With Olive, 1953
Audley Hall Mill, Blackburn
Arthur, Pearl, Dennis, Sheila and Alan at the dancing
    academy, 1956
Arthur
Olive
Raymond
Eileen on her wedding day in 1961
Alan in 1982
Alan and Kathleen with baby Grant in 1968
Alan with Grant at nine months
Grant with four-week-old Marcia
Alan at the typewriter
Alan teaching at Oliver Wells School
The Counsell family, 1982

Preface

Whenever I first meet people I realize that they need time to get used to my impeded speech. They usually have to concentrate hard to make sense of what they hear and they very soon become aware of my unsophisticated language. This is due to an inability to speak and an absence of formal speech training when I was young. The reader will soon learn how this has affected my expression and writing.

In essence this is the story of my life, but a few details have been altered for various reasons, not least where my memory has proved unreliable or for the sake of simplicity. I have also changed one or two names to protect those whose feelings might otherwise have been hurt.

Most books have a dedication and a list of 'thank yous' but it would be difficult to name and thank everyone who has helped me. However, I would be mean not to mention some of them. I had the most wonderful parents. It seems that they were singled out for me and I thank them for giving me birth and for supporting me through the many trials of growing up. I was three years old before any grunt I made was remotely intelligible to them. No other couple could have done for me what they did.

My brothers and sister were wonderful too. I thank them not just for the good things they did for me but also for caring enough to be cruel at times so that I might become less selfish and more self-reliant. I include in my thanks their husband and wives.

A special thanks to my three children. To Grant for being so sensible and mature. The other week I had to visit his school and address his class. I was worried in case his school friends might give him a bad time because of my speech and appearance. When this possibility was discussed with him he shocked me by his philosophy. 'You are my dad. If anyone says anything to me about you I will ask them if *their* dad could do as well as you if he had your problems.' No matter how difficult things may be I feel I have to go on making progress just to live up to Grant's expectations.

Thank you, Marcia and Emma, for being so loving. Your cuddles brighten my life, your optimism always encourages me.

Thanks go to Susan Hill of Hutchinson for her constant patience, enthusiasm, encouragement and advice, and without whom this book could never have been completed.

A problem becomes less important and easier to overcome when it is shared. All my family have shared my problem and made my life easier through that sharing. My handicap is nothing more than another problem with another solution. The solution is Kathleen. I sometimes wonder where I would be today without my wife. I do not know the source of her patience and tolerance. During our fifteen years of marriage she has cared for me in every situation. I am the man that she has made. She is my friend, my counsellor, my companion and my confidante. Without her I would indeed be handicapped.

1

I know every peel of paint, every tattered magazine in this waiting room because I wait here every Wednesday evening and have done so for the past four years. Tonight I am determined that Dr Mack will tell me what is wrong with me. I feel so tense and aggressive that I am impatient for the other four patients to go on into the surgery.

I wonder what they are thinking as they sit there looking at me. I wonder how I appear to them. How noticeable is my handicap? Do they wonder what is actually wrong with me?

Every Wednesday I sit in this clinical waiting room, on the same chilly brown leather seat, and stare at the pale walls until all the other patients have seen the doctor, until at last it is my turn. Dr Mack likes me to be his final patient and we sit together in his surgery and talk, sometimes for as long as an hour. The chats we have are usually helpful and interesting but I never like the wait. It seems to me that the other patients in the waiting room stare especially hard at me today and I feel more self-conscious than ever.

For several weeks now I have been asking the doctor to explain what really is wrong with me, and the more he refuses the more resentful I become and the more determined I am to find out. Tonight I am going to demand that Dr Mack tells me about myself. After all I am eighteen and I feel it's about time I knew the truth. I can understand my parents not really knowing because they have always accepted what Dr Mack has said for all these years, but I am sure there must be a proper name for my condition and I desperately want to know exactly what is the matter. Dr Mack has always said to my parents that I will grow out of whatever it is and that as

I get older I will improve, but I am sure he could tell me a lot more. Tonight I am going to insist that he tells me everything. Each muscle in my body seems clenched.

The last patient is tapping on the door as she is leaving the surgery, which indicates that the doctor is ready for me.

I knock on the inner door and hear Dr Mack's fine Scottish voice bidding me to enter. I am so taut that I feel ready to spring at him but I am disarmed as he greets me in his usual friendly manner. 'Good evening Alan, everyone else gone? Come and sit down.'

I usually sit in the chair opposite him but tonight I am too intent on my purpose to sit down. My anxiety comes out in an angry rush.

'Doctor, I demand to know what is wrong with me. I have been asking you for weeks and I do not think you know. If you do not know, I would like to see some other doctor who could tell me. If you do know, then I insist that you tell me.'

I have to stop for breath and as I look down at Dr Mack's white hair my gaze is carried to his eyes and I know from his look that my determination has registered. He answers me in a much quieter voice than he normally uses. 'Sit down and we will talk about it.'

I take a chair and wait. I can see that the doctor is thinking carefully about his next words. 'Why are you so intent on knowing what is wrong with you?'

'I just want to know.' He smiles at me in a way which makes me feel uneasy. 'Doctor, wouldn't you want to know in my position?'

He says nothing but nods his head reluctantly. There is silence, then Dr Mack stands and begins to pace the room. He looks thoughtful.

'All right, I will tell you,' he says as he goes back to his leather swivel chair. 'I suppose it could be my fault that you are the way you are, but who can tell?' He hesitates, then continues. 'I will start at the beginning. When your mother was carrying you, she would be about seven months pregnant I think, she fell down the stairs at home. She didn't tell me at the time, but after the fall she did not feel you move very much. You were your mother's sixth baby and as she

10

had already had five births without any trouble at all I thought everything would be all right with yours as well. I used to see your mother every week at the end of her pregnancy but I never examined her. I used to ask her if everything was all right and because she had had so many babies I trusted her replies when she said she felt quite normal.' Mother was forty-one when I was born.

The doctor exchanges glances with me and continues. 'When labour began I found you were lying the wrong way round. You were going to be born breech and I could not turn you.'

I am interrupting the doctor.

'What is breech?'

'A baby is usually born head first. You were clearly going to be born bottom first. That is called a breech birth.' He stops talking and looks at me as though he is trying to read the reactions on my face. 'Had I examined your mother before she went into labour I could have turned you to the correct position but it was too late by then.'

'Is this why you say that it could be your fault that I am the way I am? I do not understand.'

'Yes, Alan, I should have examined your mother and maybe I could have prevented a difficult birth. Although one cannot be absolutely sure, that slip could have been the cause of your handicap.'

Again he looks at me as though he is searching my face to make sure I am not too distressed or upset. He continues. 'When labour ended and you were finally born you were very weak and would not breathe. I put my mouth over your nose and mouth and gently blew into your lungs. I had never done that to a baby before. After a few minutes you began breathing for yourself but I was not happy with your condition and ordered alternate hot and cold baths for you, hoping that this would save you. Within an hour you had stopped breathing and again I tried to revive you by breathing into you. You responded well and within a few moments you were breathing on your own. But still I was not happy about you and I had to tell your mother and father that you might not live. They sent for a minister and had you

11

christened in the bedroom. One of your uncles and one of your aunts and the man who lived next door were there to witness the christening and as you were laid down after the ceremony you stopped breathing yet again and this time it took about five minutes to revive you. You were so weak I did not think you would live. The midwife and I continued to give you hot and cold baths, and your father worked very hard boiling lots of water for us. Your mother was terribly distressed and the situation was awful, with all of us in the same room as your mother because it was the only one in the whole house with a fire to heat it. You seemed to be recovering and had been sleeping for about two hours when the midwife saw that you had stopped breathing again. I tried to revive you but it took a long time. I was about to give up but finally you did start to breathe. I thought you were too weak to live and wondered how long we were going to go on reviving you like that. You were sleeping rather restlessly when you suddenly started to cry. You had been born fifteen hours by then but that was the first time you had cried. I knew when I heard you cry that you were going to be all right because to cry the way you did you needed to use your lungs to their full capacity.'

I feel a little impatient and I interrupt, 'This is all very interesting but you are not telling me what is wrong with me.'

I think the doctor is irritated by my interruption but he answers calmly. 'I am trying to tell you in a way that you will understand. So please listen to me.'

There is another pause and the doctor looks at me as though he is expecting me to argue. 'I had no idea that you would be handicapped. I thought I had kept you breathing sufficiently well by using my own breath to save you from damage.'

The word damage alarms me and I repeat it cautiously. 'Damage?'

'Yes, Alan, you are brain-damaged. That is what is wrong with you.'

There is silence and I think the doctor is trying to assess my reaction.

My thoughts race ahead of my reason and I am trying to

12

figure it out in my own mind. Brain damage. Is he trying to tell me now, after all that I have been through, that I am mental?

'Doctor, I do not understand what you are saying. How can I be brain-damaged. I am not mental. Please explain just what you mean.'

Something about Dr Mack's expression makes me think he expected this kind of response. 'No, Alan, you are not mental. It is your brain's motor system that's damaged, not your intellect.'

There is another pause and I look closely at him and feel a bit comforted although I still don't really understand. I have grown used to his stern but sympathetic manner and I feel confidence in him. The doctor has been a part of my life for as long as I can remember; surely I can trust him?

'This is all very confusing to me,' I tell him.

'Of course it is. I am going to explain further and you will understand better when I have finished.'

I notice that the palms of my hands are hot and clammy, in fact I feel flushed and hot. I am not sure whether I feel excited or frightened or both. I sit back in my chair to show I am willing to listen to whatever he has to say, and Dr Mack continues.

'The brain is made up of tiny cells which need oxygen to function. Each of these cells controls some aspect of your body. If these cells are deprived of oxygen, even for a short time, they do not work as they should and they become damaged. I suspect that when you had difficulty breathing after you were born some of your brain cells were damaged through lack of oxygen. The damaged cells in your case, affect your movements, your arms, legs and speech. This is a very simple explanation of what is wrong with you. It will be a little difficult for you to understand but if you would like to ask me any questions I will try to answer them.'

'Why haven't you told me this before? Why don't my parents know?'

'I have never put a label on you because people react to labels and I wanted you to be treated normally or as normally as possible. You see, Alan, even you, earlier in our conversation, reacted to the word "damage" by thinking you were mental and that is what I have tried to discourage others from doing all your life. You cannot walk properly and you cannot use your hands very well. You have a lot of uncontrollable shakes and facial movements and of course you have difficulty with your speech. Whenever anyone has asked your parents what was wrong with you this is what they have been told. It is enough for the majority of people, they accept it without any further explanation. If they have wanted to know more we have told them that you were born like that and that in time you might improve.'

I feel stunned. I feel a bit stupid, and I cannot yet comprehend that there is something wrong with my brain. I'd always thought that the brain related to intellect, to being clever or dim, daft or mental, but never to the ability to walk or talk.

The doctor's voice breaks through my thoughts. 'Now Alan, do you understand all that I have said?'

'I don't know, doctor. I feel confused. I did not know that the brain controlled our walking and talking. I thought if you had something wrong with your brain you were mental.'

'No, no, it's not like that at all. This is what most people think. I am sure you have seen puppets, haven't you? Well, you are like a puppet with your brain pulling the strings. Some of your strings are knotted or stretched so that when they are pulled, the part of the body which responds doesn't move as it should. Does that make it easier to understand?'

'Yes, I think so, but I did not expect you to say that there was something wrong with my brain when I asked you what was wrong with me.'

'Just what did you expect? What did you think was wrong with you?'

'I thought it was something to do with my nerves, because of my shakes and trembles.'

'What do you mean by nerves?'

'I don't really know.'

'People use the word "nerves" and often don't understand the meaning of it. There is nothing wrong with your nerves. What you have is something which is called cerebral palsy.

14

Cerebral means to do with the brain and palsy means a paralysis. In common language, you are a spastic.'

Now this I cannot accept, and after all my efforts to remain calm and demonstrate control, I finally feel anger welling up.

'Spastic! How can I be a spastic? Everyone knows spastics are imbecciles in wheelchairs. How can I be a spastic?' I know I am shouting at the doctor.

'Alan, you are reacting exactly like the ill-informed majority of people. The words "spastic" and "brain damage" are very emotive because people don't fully understand their meaning. Because your body doesn't function normally and your speech is impaired and because people mistake you for mental, as you describe it, doesn't mean you are. You wanted to know what was wrong with you and I have told you. I am prepared to answer all the questions you want to ask. I don't want you to leave me tonight until you are happy about what I have said to you.'

We went on for a long time. The doctor told me more about the night of my birth, how my sister Olive, who was only a child, had run the house for a while afterwards, and how he himself had never charged my parents a penny for his work that night or any of his many subsequent visits. I think he felt as terrible as I did. It would, he said, have taken my parents the rest of their lives to pay the accounts.

'No matter what I have said, you are still the same person who came in here earlier this evening. The only difference is that now you have a little more knowledge about yoourself,' said Dr Mack at the end of our talk.

As I am leaving the surgery to walk home I begin to think how lucky I am, because from what the doctor has said, I could after the circumstances of my birth have been very much more helpless and handicapped, but my brain was not damaged to that extent.

I wonder how my family would have reacted to me if they had known that I was brain-damaged. I can begin to see now how wise the doctor has been not to put a label on me.

I am as I am and a lot of effort on the part of many people has made me what I finally am. Such reflections lead me to think about my life and all that has happened to me.

15

2

The room looks so cosy in the dim glow of the dying embers of the fire which has kept the bedroom warm during the night and although outside the morning is cold, it is comfortable as I lie here in my bed looking at the familiar shadows and silhouettes cast by the furniture on the walls of the room.

The silence of the early morning is broken by the sound of my father whistling in the bakehouse next door. He owns the bakehouse and works there every day. The banging of the rings, which are used to shape the crumpets, and the sound of my mother's clogs on the stone floor bring to my mind a picture of father pouring batter into the rings on the hotplate while mother packs the crumpets which have cooled into large baskets ready for father to take round to his customers later. I know too that grandfather has arrived at the bakehouse to begin his work, for the solo whistling is now a vigorous duet in the huge, dimly lit room.

Just before seven o'clock every morning grandfather arrives from his home in Withers Street, having been followed down Alker Street by the family cat. He will take over from mother so that she can attend to the family. Grandfather will be giving my younger brother, Tom, a little attention as he watches the bustle from his pram. The baby has recently developed the habit of waking early, before mother can give him any time, and so he is taken into the bakehouse until grandfather arrives and mother is free for him.

Mother will have been in the bakehouse since about four o'clock this morning. Her hair will be neatly plaited into a bun at the back of her head. Her hair is so long that when it is

16

loose she is able to sit on it. I can picture her, slight in her print apron, as she moves energetically around the bakehouse packing crumpets and washing the huge earthenware containers which have been emptied of batter as father worked through the night. Mother has always been used to hard work, as she was a weaver before she married twenty years ago. She is a young-looking woman in spite of her forty-four years.

Father will be dressed in his white hat and apron and the sweat will be glistening on his brow as he stands over the hotplate performing the different manoeuvres with skilled precision. He has worked in the bakehouse since he came out of the army twenty-two years ago. Grandfather owned the bakehouse until recently but he is now semi-retired because of his health. The family crumpet-baking business is now in its fourth generation, and we have always lived in the working-class district of Audley, in the Lancashire mill town of Blackburn.

Another day is awakening; the sound of weavers' clogs from the street below blends with the voice of my mother as she rouses my sister, Olive, and chides her to prepare for her work in a baker's shop on Copy Nook. Soon the real shouting will begin as mother tries to wake my brothers who sleep in the same room as me. 'John, Joe, come along. Time to get up.' The homely clatter of breakfast being prepared in the kitchen is mingled with more loud calls. 'John, Joe, come on! I won't tell you again, time to be up.'

The whistling from the bakehouse has stopped. This usually means that father will be coming into the house and heaven help John and Joe if they are still in bed. How I wish that I could join my brothers as they leave their beds and scamper down to the kitchen to wash and then rush back to the bedroom to dress. How I wish that I could walk.

'John, get a move on. You know what will happen if this fire isn't lit for Alan by the time your father comes in.'

Not surprisingly rude comments are flung at me as my brothers dress but I just wait there for my father to come up and carry me downstairs, wrapped in my blanket, and lay me on the sofa in the living room. I spend a little time each day

17

on the sofa in the comfort of my blanket, watching the family. I look forward to them all being together in the morning and the evening. They really are my whole world because I don't have any friends or playmates. I cannot walk so I stay indoors with my mother. Even if I were able to go out and play the children would not understand my speech.

My father and grandfather have resumed their whistling in the bakehouse and their rendition of 'Happy birthday to you' reminds me that this, 11 November 1942, is my fifth birthday. Olive says I still looked like a rag doll.

It is a custom in our house that each child is allowed to pick up the post from the lobby on their birthday. Our front door is always open and the postman never uses the letter box. He just opens the vestibule door and throws our mail down the hall. I wonder if there is some way I could pick up my own post today. As my father carries me downstairs I ask him. 'Could I please pick up my own birthday cards today?'

It is no good. Why, oh why, can father never tell what I say? The words are so clear in my mind. Why does father always have to answer so inappropriately. I try again. 'No, I'm not asking if John will have time to feed me this morning. I just want to pick up my cards.'

Why does father have to quarrel with mother and shout at John each time I speak to him? Of course he is not the only one who cannot tell what I say. No one ever answers me correctly, and yet the words are so clear in my mind.

Mother is always busy; she runs the house, caring for all seven of us, and she does a great deal of work in the bakehouse. Often she takes care of sick neighbours as well. If John does not have time to feed me before he goes to school I have to wait for mother to finish with the new baby. It takes a long time to feed me and the baby cries if he is kept waiting, so he is fed first. I just wait in my blanket on the sofa. I don't think John likes feeding me and I don't enjoy him doing it, anyway. I cannot swallow my food very well and I easily choke. I usually dribble most of what is put in my mouth back out. Of all my brothers and sisters, Olive is the best at feeding me because she is never in a hurry and puts small amounts of food into my mouth; she also holds the

18

empty spoon under my lip and pushes back what I dribble out. Mother is always kind to me and is by far the best at feeding me but she says it's a full-time job and cannot do it all the time. Lots of neighbours try to help with my feeding but they do not understand what it feels like to have food crammed into your mouth when you can't swallow it. Some of them like to tip my head back to prevent the food from dribbling out and often I have to hit out at people with my arms as I cannot breathe because of the mashed-up stuff being pushed relentlessly into my mouth. Olive says I nearly died again and again as a baby because I could not take milk, or any other food, until father invented a method of giving me milk from an eye-dropper.

Lunchtime is extremely busy as my brothers come home from school to eat and the baby needs feeding too. Very often Uncle Bob, who is a family friend, or Mammy Buck, a neighbour, will come in and try to help mother by feeding me.

Aunty Elsie, father's sister, comes to see me once or twice a week. I like her. She is always affectionate and cheerful, and her skin seems clean and shiny. She lives with my grandmother and I feel I am very special to her, just as she is to me. I call her my sunshine aunty because she is always so warm towards me and when she takes me on her lap it is lovely to be held with such obvious fondness. Aunty Elsie will often feed me my meals and I always enjoy that enormously. I feel quite comfortable on her lap even though she is thin. Usually thin people are uncomfortable to sit on.

As I am now five there is a lot of talk in the family about me going to school. My mother must have sent a letter to the headmistress this morning with my brothers, for they have brought a letter back from school this afternoon. I have to go and see the headmistress tomorrow. I am not looking forward to meeting her, as the rest of the family talk about her as though she is terrible. Anyway, I don't really want to go to school.

Mother is unusually affectionate as she wheels me in my pushchair to the school, but she sounds as though she would really like me to go there like other children. She has

19

promised that we can wait for my brothers to come out from their classes after we have seen the headmistress. She is quite tall and she kind of leans to one side as she walks. She is wearing a green two-piece and she is taking us to her office. She seems nice; I think I like her. Mother is sitting at the opposite side of the desk but I am sitting by the headmistress, who has pulled a leaf from her desk and gives me some paper to draw on. Mother is looking angry. I don't know why, because the headmistress is not upsetting *me* by saying she can't take me into her school. I do not want to go there anyway. Apparently the school would not be able to cope with me because I need to be carried everywhere and the head thinks that I will not be bright enough to understand the work and the lessons.

I am looking forward to going home with my brothers. I wonder if I will have to ride home in my pushchair or whether John will give me a piggyback as father does when we go to the park.

After a little while we leave the school and when we arrive home mother is relating the events to Mammy Buck, who has been looking after the baby. Mammy Buck is as indignant as mother. I feel sure that father is going to be very angry when he hears what has been said at the school. My parents want me to go to the same local school as my brothers because the doctor thinks I may overcome my problems more easily if I am treated just like every other member of the family, so I guess father will take me to see the doctor this evening to get advice about my schooling.

Just as I expected, father is furious. The doctor advises that I should be kept at home until I am allowed to go to school with my brothers.

Most evenings Olive puts me to bed and I love this as she sings to me or recites nursery rhymes. Mother is always busy with Tom at this time but I do not mind. I like to be with Olive, she always smells of perfume and wears make-up to make herself look nice.

It is wartime and I hate it when the air-raid sirens go off in the night and wake me up, but Olive always carries me in my blanket to the shelter in the back yard which we share with the people next door, Mammy and Pappy Earnshaw. It is built of thick concrete with sandbags stacked around the outside. When we are all inside father and Pappy always barricade the door with bags before father goes off to do his job as an air-raid warden. We are only allowed a very small light in the shelter and we sing songs or nursery rhymes. Mammy Earnshaw always brings a flask of hot chocolate into the shelter and shares it with us. They have a dog which usually lies trembling under one of the seats. My sister always takes care of me while we are there and mother holds Tom. We often hear the bombs dropping and feel the vibrations from their blasts. Usually in the morning life goes along in the routine way.

Time has passed and here I am sitting under the living-room table bawling loudly, having dropped a cob of coal on my hand and gashed my finger open as I crawled past the coal scuttle which mother had left at the top of the lobby when she went to answer a knocking on the front door. Who is this man? He is wearing a trilby hat and carrying a briefcase. My mother is telling him I won't go to any school other than the one my brothers go to. I do not like this man, for had he not come mother would have bandaged my finger. The man is a school inspector. I have a feeling that when my father is told of this visit, he will fly into a temper and then it will be yet another visit to the doctor.

What jubilation there is in our home today. I have not heard anything about my going to school for a few weeks, but a letter came this morning and it seems I am to go along to school with my brothers next Monday. Father is very pleased although my brothers John and Joe are not happy at the prospect of carrying me there and back and seeing to me at playtime, which father says they must do.

I do not share the rest of the family's excitement about my starting school. I had to be up earlier this morning as it is my first day. Mother got me ready and brought me along in the pushchair with my teddy and now I am in the classroom with my teacher and all the other children. The classroom is very big with lots of tiny tables and chairs. There are nice pictures on the walls and a carpet in one corner of the room. Miss Groom is my teacher, and she is tall and thin with blonde hair like my sister's. She is friendly and keeps asking me if I am all right. She has put me on the carpet with my teddy. I felt frightened on my way here and my brothers quarrelled this morning because Joe says he does not know how he can manage to carry me, my teddy and my gas mask home, but now that I have met my teacher I feel better. She has a soft, kind face. At playtime Joe takes me to the toilet and carries me into the girls' playground. The teacher thought the girls would be gentler to me than the boys, who can be rough and might hurt me. When we get into the playground my grandmother is waiting at the railings. She has come to make sure I am all right and she passes some sweets for me through the railings while I sit on the grass.

I have now been at school for a few days and there is a big girl who collects me and takes me to the toilet at playtime and gives me my milk from a bottle with a teat because I cannot manage to drink through a straw. Sometimes my grandmother waits outside by the railings and she gives me my milk. I prefer grandmother to give it to me because she covers me with newspaper so I do not get my front all wet as I drink. Going to the toilet is difficult because I need help. The big girl, who has become my friend, only takes me to the toilet at playtime; if I want to go during lessons the teacher has to send for my brother, who grumbles venomously about this as well as about carrying me home.

Miss Groom has asked Joe to tell her the special signs and noises which the family recognize as meaning something whenever I make them. I try to speak but apparently the words are not recognizable to others, so when I say, 'I want a drink,' and things like that, my family recognize the noise rather than the words. Although I am unable to speak properly, my family have taken a lot of trouble to teach me the names of things and have given me an idea of how to form language. The noises I make are my attempts to repeat words back to them. I have been taught the names for everything around me; I know, for example, that a table is a table and my family have tried to get me to say the word 'table'. The sound I make, although it doesn't sound like 'table', communicates to them what I mean. I have quite an extensive vocabulary of sounds because my family constantly talk to me and get me to make noises. Unfortunately these noises are often meaningless to anyone but me. Even my family are only able to understand some of them; they remember the noises for the important words, like 'toilet', 'hungry' and 'thirsty'. It is still mysterious to me that each time I say a word it sounds clear in my mind but is not intelligible to anyone else. I can't wait to grow up because the doctor says I will get better, but sometimes I wonder.

So now Miss Groom is trying to learn to recognize some of my sounds and I feel a bit more comfortable at school.

In my second class I am expected to write, which is very difficult. I am often upset by the teacher, Miss Jones, who says that I am messy and by the children, who take the mickey out of me because I use two hands to hold the pencil, while they are able to manage with one. Sometimes they laugh at me when I speak to them because they say I shake and I talk funny and they can't tell what I am saying, but I don't know why. The words are so clear in my mind. I don't like Miss Jones. She has black hair and she wears glasses. She does not seem to smile much. Many of the other children don't like her either. We all liked Miss Groom – she was kind – but we think Miss Jones is horrible. She tells me off for not walking and she won't let my brother in the classroom to take me to the toilet, so I keep wetting myself because she can't tell when I am asking to go. Nor will she take me there herself. She refuses to carry me and I have to crawl around the school. When I go home with wet trousers mother is angry and smacks me and does not understand when I tell her about the teacher. I would say it was frustrating if I could have used or formulated or understood such a word then. Miss Jones says I am either lazy or backward and if I am just lazy it won't help me if she does everything for me and if I am backward I should be in a school for retarded children, and she is going to have me sent there if necessary.

23

The headteacher has given me a letter to take home. Father is reading it and I can tell by his face that he is not happy. In fact I have never seen him so angry. He has put his fist through the wooden back door. There is something dreadfully wrong because as father is carrying me to the doctor he is crying and hugging me tightly. I can see the tears in his eyes and he is too upset to talk to me. We are in the surgery and father is growing more and more tense. That letter must be really important. Now father is further worried because the doctor thinks we ought to have a solicitor and father says he has not got enough money to pay for one. Apparently the education authority wants to place me in a school for the mentally defective and the only way this can be prevented is by having a solicitor who can take our case to a special kind of court. Now that we have returned home from the doctor, father is saying that I am not to go to school but I am to stay at home until this is all sorted out. I stay away from school for eight months.

Grandfather has given money to pay a solicitor to prove I am not 'feeble-minded' as they say. They also say my spine is so weak I will never walk.

My mother has a friend who lives opposite us. She is small and white-haired and she makes hats. She often pops into our house and I call her Mammy Brogden. While I am away from school she and Mammy Earnshaw, from next door, are teaching me to read and write. I like it better than going to school. Sometimes they both come to my house and other times I am taken to one of their homes. This is a lovely time for me. Each day grandmother comes and takes me out in my pushchair. She wraps me in a huge white towel and gives me ice cream. She always says the ice cream is our secret and that I am not to tell my brothers. When grandmother talks to me it is in a different way from anyone else as though, unlike other people, she knows that I understand what she is saying. Grandmother also understands a little of what I say to her. So, nowadays, does mother, although I have to repeat it.

Every Thursday I go to grandmother's and she makes me leek soup for lunch because it's my favourite, and no one can make leek soup like she does. We also go shopping at the

24

Co-op next door to her house. Thursday is half-day closing and we always wait until all the other customers have gone before we go in. The manager, Billy, lets me help him count the money and weigh out some of the things that grandmother is buying. He also gets me to spin coins on the counter, as he says it might help to get my fingers working. When we leave the shop I always pull down the blind on the door as Billy lifts me up to reach it. We lock the door and Billy holds grandmother's bags while she carries me.

In the meantime the solicitor has been to our home several times. He seems a nice man and always wears a smart suit. He does not speak with an accent like us, but with an educated voice. My mother says he does not come from Lancashire. He has a car and leaves it outside our front door. If he arrives when the children are not at school they all come to look at the car as though they had never seen one before. Each time the solicitor comes he takes papers out of his case and asks lots of questions. He does not speak to me – just to my parents – but I listen and watch from the sofa. Today's visit seems to be special and the solicitor has sent for Mammy Earnshaw and Mammy Brogden. He is concerned because I have to go and meet a group of people who will ask me lots of questions. The solicitor is worried because he does not think that these people will understand my replies and he is asking if I might be able to answer in writing instead. I cannot understand why the solicitor is worried because when I speak, the words are quite clear to me. Mammy Earnshaw and Mammy Brogden are saying that given my own time I will be able to write the answers to the questions. The solicitor is now asking me to write my name for him but I'm afraid he does not seem very impressed, although he pats me on the head and tells me I'm a good boy.

The day has arrived when we are to meet these people who seem to matter so much. It is a special occasion. I can tell because mother and father are wearing their Sunday clothes and I have to wear a bib to protect my new, clean jersey from my constant and uncontrollable flow of dribble. Mother does not like my jersey because grandmother bought it for me. Father says that he does not know how grandmother got my

25

jersey without clothing coupons. It irritates my mother that grandmother is often able to supply many of the things which I need when she herself can't. I suspect that mother feels she should be the one to supply my needs. But we are quite poor and mother has a large family, while grandmother's children have all grown up so she can spoil me a little. Grandmother also has a lot more time than mother, who I know is a bit envious of the hours grandmother spends with me.

Dr Mack, who is taking us to our meeting in his car, has just arrived. The atmosphere has suddenly become charged with excitement as mother and I are ushered into the back of the car. The leather seat is cold and slippery and the doctor is trying to make me comfortable by placing his overcoat under and around me. He says that this will make it more safe for me while we are travelling. I have never been in a car before and mother has her arm around me to keep me steady against the funny, unfamiliar jogging.

As we travel she keeps reminding me that this is an important time and I must promise to do my very best to do all that the people ask of me. Mother is telling me that these people want to find out how clever I really am.

We arrive at a large building in a big town and father is carrying me up a long, long staircase and into a large room which has a table at one end with chairs around it. Never in the whole of my seven years have I seen a room as big; it seems to me to be a colossal and frightening expanse of empty space. I feel small and afraid. When father sits me on a chair and leaves me in the centre of the room I am terrified, lost and forlorn until the doctor and my father join me and stand on each side of me. The solicitor joins us and is shaking hands with my father and the doctor. He shakes my hand too but I feel rather uncomfortable about this as I am not able to open my right hand and the solicitor has to take my whole fist into his grasp.

A lot of people are entering the room. They also seem to be dressed in their Sunday best. They look dignified and I think they are probably posh people. As they all enter the room my wet, soggy bib is whipped from me and stuffed into my father's pocket. The solicitor is sitting at one end of the

26

long, polished table and is talking to the other people around it.

The doctor and my father are answering questions and I am being asked to write my name and draw various shapes. I have to recognize different coins and say what coin has the biggest value. I am being asked the date and what year it is. One gentleman has emptied his pockets of money and is asking me to count it. I am asked lots of questions and when anyone cannot tell what I say they ask my father or the doctor to interpret, and if even then they are unable to understand me I have to write down what I want to say. I know this makes things more complicated because my writing is almost as difficult to understand as my speech.

I think we have been in the room half an hour or so but now at the end of the ordeal mother and father seem well pleased. Dr Mack is speaking to my father. 'I knew he had it in him. I felt it was right to go ahead.'

I don't really know what it all means but my praises are sung all the way home in the car and it is obvious that the three adults think I am rather clever.

As we arrive home the neighbours all come out of their houses to greet us and many of them are crowding around the car asking mother how we got on. Then they are hugging and kissing me and I don't know what's come over them. My grandmother is waiting inside the house with Mammy Earnshaw and Mammy Brogden and they are trying to read a piece of paper which father is waving about.

Grandmother is the first to speak to me. 'We will show them, Alan. You're not daft and this proves it. No one can argue with this.'

She flaps the paper at me and father joins in the excitement. 'Listen Alan, this paper says that today Alan Counsell has been found to have an above average intelligence and to be of sane mind. This means you will be able to go to school with your brothers.'

I have mixed feelings about this. First, I didn't mind not going to school, but mainly I dwell on the words which grandmother has said. I have never thought before that people might think I was daft. That's what they meant by

27

mental defective. I do not understand. I somehow link being thought daft with my inability to walk and I decide I shall refuse to be carried again. I must walk. I really must.

When I return to school and I refuse to be carried, there are problems because I cannot walk and I am not being wheeled either. The only way mother can get me to go to school is suspended between my brother and his friend. My eldest brother, John, has left school and is working, so is no longer able to help me in this. Mother is terribly cross because of the state of my clog toes. They are badly scuffed and scraped because of the way I am dragged to school each day. I don't care. I am not being carried and I am determined that I shall learn how to walk. My brother thinks that dragging me to school is ridiculous and he is giving me a bad time. He does not understand when I try to explain that I would rather try to use my legs than be carried. It is frustrating to try to argue with him for he seems not to know what I am trying to say. Sometimes when I speak to Joe he will mimic me and I must say that he sounds as though he is grunting rather than speaking. I would love to know how I really sound to people when I speak to them. I cannot participate in long conversations and usually my family just ask me questions which demand a yes or no answer. That way I can shake or nod my head. But when I actually say something to them they rarely understand me.

After a few weeks of struggling to school between my brother and his friend, I feel more aware of what my legs should be doing. I am sure if I can get Joe to slow down I could take a few proper steps. At last, after days of trying, I have got this through to Joe and manage a few steps while he and his friend are holding on to me. It is hard to make them understand what I want. I have to pull on their necks to get them to slow down. Then I put all my weight on them and all my concentration into my mime, and they finally see my efforts at walking and understand what I want them to do. No one is more excited than Joe, who cannot wait to tell mother. This is a major breakthrough because now that Joe has seen my attempts to walk he is more enthusiastic about helping me.

28

Of course the doctor has to be consulted, but to my surprise he does not give any hope of further progress and is afraid that I might injure myself in my efforts. I don't understand how he can say that I will grow out of whatever is wrong with me if he is now saying that I should not be trying to walk. How will I grow out of it if I am not allowed to attempt to do the things I feel I should be doing? Dr Mack says that I should leave walking for at least another five years but I am not daunted and insist that Joe and his friend continue to help. My only aid in winning any argument is my ability to scream. Joe cannot bear my tantrums and I know that through them I can get him to encourage me. Of course I can only take a very few steps and then only when I am supported on both sides, but I feel I am making progress.

Very soon Aunty Elsie and her friend Maggie become my allies and spend time with me at the weekends, allowing me to use their arms as parallel bars to support myself while I practise my walking. They sit opposite each other holding hands with their arms extended and I walk from one to the other. My brother John and sister Olive have also joined forces and are helping me each evening before I go to bed by letting me walk between their arms just like aunty and her friend do. The doctor is still pessimistic but I am making advances with the help of my family. After all, without them I wouldn't even be able to stand. Everyone else has always been so pessimistic about me.

Miss Cook, my current teacher, is very supportive too and is doing all she can. She walks with me every time I need to go to the toilet and props me from behind with her hands under my armpits. She is a serious-looking woman and does not smile much, but all the class like her. She never shouts like some of the other teachers do, but we do as we are told.

Another few weeks have passed and I am now able to walk around my home and classroom holding on to the furniture. My parents are forced to admit that I really am going to walk but they are apprehensive and consult the doctor again.

Dr Mack confesses that he never expected me to stand on my own let alone walk and as I have made so much progress without doing any damage to myself, maybe I could be encouraged and helped a little more.

My parents, after initial unease, now involve themselves in my learning to walk and I am allowed to use the bakehouse for practising. It is a terraced building at the end of a row and all the inside walls on the ground floor have been knocked out, so there is a lot of space. It is now one large room. What was once the back yard has been given a roof and windows; it used to be the stables for grandfather's horse in the old days, but is now incorporated into the vast floor space of the bakehouse. Down one side of the room stretches a wooden construction with a mesh top, on which crumpets are cooled after they have been baked. This is followed by a series of tables with white scrubbed tops. The crumpets are stacked here when they have cooled. This rack and the tables give me a continuous support as I try to walk the full length of the bakehouse. The more progress I make the keener my family become. My legs are massaged every morning and evening, and luckily for me someone is always willing to drop what they are doing whenever I want to practise.

At school there is a corridor which runs the full length of the building with the girls' toilets at one end and the boys' at the other. My classroom is nearer the girls' and I have to use it, as I cannot yet walk the distance to the boys' toilet. I hate this as some of the girls laugh at me if they see me there. But I can't get to the boys' toilets without the help of Miss Cook and she is too busy to walk with me all that way. My brother is now in senior school so he can't help either. I am determined to take myself to the boys' lavatory. The first time I manage this I get myself stuck. My legs are like jelly and they will not carry me back. I have been away from the classroom for so long that Miss Cook has to come looking for me. I thought she might be angry but as she carries me back, she says that I have done well.

It is now two weeks ago since I made it one way to the toilet. Today I made it there and back on my own. The whole class is cheering but this is soon stopped by the appearance of the headmistress, who has come to see what all the noise is about.

30

To get to school I have only one busy road to cross and this runs across the bottom of our street. After this there are four side streets, and between two of these there is a long stretch of pavement which I would like to walk down on my own. Although I am making progress I go very slowly. If I don't hang on to someone's arm when I am walking outside I fall down easily, so I still need Joe to walk with me. If I do fall I cannot get up without help. Fortunately my school and Joe's school are in the same grounds so he is still able to take me there.

We are late for school this morning because I have tried to walk all the way without holding on to Joe. He is worried about what our teachers might say but now that we have arrived everything is all right. The teachers are simply saying that if I am going to walk to school we must leave home earlier. I still need Joe in case I fall because I don't have the strength in my legs to get up on my own. The other day Joe left me and went off with his friends. He said that I would be all right, but I fell down and I had to crawl almost all the way home. No one was there to help me and some children laughed, but when I came to the busy road Joe was waiting and he helped me the rest of the way home.

Joe is marvellous. I am laughed at many times in school by some of the children, who mimic the way I talk and walk, and comment on the way I write. I am not hurt by being laughed at; it's always been a part of my life and I'm used to it, but I do feel a clown when others watch those who make fun of me. When Joe is around I don't seem to be laughed at or mimicked.

Olive and father argue a lot about her desire to go dancing. Father forbids her to go to dance halls, but most evenings she gives me her dancing shoes to hide in the pig bin, left over from the war years, at the bottom of the street. Everybody throws their kitchen waste into it. Olive tells my parents she is going to visit her friend and then picks her shoes out of the bin as she passes. I am paid a penny to do this – a halfpenny to do the job and the other halfpenny not to tell anyone.

Things are different now that I can walk. I used to sit on the doorstep at the front of our house and watch the other children playing in the street, but now I can join in some of their games providing I can keep up. Recently a group of us climbed into the churchyard at the bottom of the street. Joe had to help me climb over the railings but when a policeman came they all ran and left me, and the policemen had to get me out. I am surprised to find that my father knows about this incident; apparently all the policemen on our beat visit him during the night while he is at work in the bakehouse.

Now that I am able to play in the street I am getting to know other children, although it is difficult to have a conversation with them. I feel awkward when I am with them and I feel I would be left out of their games if it were not for my brothers. I would like to make friends with the other children but don't know how. It is the same at school now that I am allowed to play in the boys' playground; I feel strange as I have been used to being with one special friend in the girls' playground, and I would like to make friends with the boys but don't know how.

I have left Miss Cook's class now and I am not happy at school. The different teachers all have conflicting ideas on how I should be treated. My new teacher, Mrs Carlisle, does everything for me, but I would rather try and do things for myself. She has arranged for a doctor who is an expert in artificial limbs to come and see me. This doctor has fitted her husband with an artificial arm after he was wounded in the war. The doctor has sent for me and I go to the head's room where she undresses me and helps me to dress again after the doctor has examined me. He is now advising that my right arm and hand should be amputated and a false one fitted instead. He also recommends that after my amputation I am educated at a school for limbless children.

My own doctor does not agree, once again, and after yet another controversy, it seems I am to remain at this school. The fact that I have been seen by a doctor without my parents' consent is causing yet another quarrel between my mother and father and the headmistress. It seems that they are to be constant enemies.

I still use two hands to hold my pencil when I write but now my writing is readable; the more I practise the better it

32

becomes. My writing is very slow and so I don't get through as much work as the rest of the children in my class, but I try my best and Mrs Carlisle seems happy with what I manage. Although I am behind with my written work I am able to keep up with the theory. Fortunately I seem to have a good memory and although I don't get much practice, I do tend to remember new learning. I do not seem to get much sympathy outside the family now. There is something appealing about a helpless baby, but a "difficult' child is quite different.

Miss Martin is my teacher this year and she is tall, fair-haired and young. She seems tense and shouts a lot. She is always complaining about the state of my jersey. I dribble profusely and the front of my sweater is hard and stained no matter how many times mother changes me. Miss Martin complains to the head who writes another letter to my mother. She ignores these letters but if father sees one he comes to school and has another argument.

There has been an appointment made for me to see an orthopaedic specialist, who seems surprised when he meets me and says that he cannot do anything but thinks that physiotherapy will help. Dr Mack does not agree, but says it can do no harm, so once a week I am to attend the clinic for various manipulations and exercises.

My mother always comes with me to the clinic every Friday morning and she has got to know the people here quite well. We have been coming for about eight weeks and one of the therapists has told my mother that the staff at the clinic are surprised at my ability, as they were given the impression from a report which was sent to them by my school that I am a low achiever. This has caused my father to turn blue with rage and once again he is visiting school. I know he is in school because I can hear him shouting as I work in the classroom. This will mean the end of my physiotherapy.

The next time father visits the school is to complain about the way I am constantly coming home from school holding up my trousers. I have never been able to do up my buttons and have always needed help. Until now a teacher has always done my buttons but my present teacher refuses. If I go to the

toilet at school I have either to find Miss Cook, who does not
mind me going to her for help, or wait for mother to do up my
buttons when I get home.

Mother is cleaning out the parlour and the living room and
making a very thorough job of it because Olive is bringing a
young man to tea on Sunday. He is called Harry and he looks
nervous as he is introduced to my parents. He is introduced
to me and turns to Olive. 'Did you say his name was Alan?'
    I don't like people who pretend I am not there and can't
ask me questions so Harry had better watch out.
    At mealtimes I like to sit by my sister when she is at home
so that she can feed me. I can swallow much better now and I
try to feed myself but my food is still mashed up for me
because I choke so easily. Today I have to sit between Olive
and Harry and I think Harry is trying to impress the family
by feeding me. He is quite good at it but why can't he ask me
what I want instead of asking Olive?
    'Olive, will Alan eat this?'
    'Olive, would Alan like some bread and butter?'
    'Olive, does Alan take sugar in his tea?'
    Anyone would think that I was unable to answer for
myself.
    Olive has just returned from work and it is the first time I
have seen her since meeting Harry yesterday.
    'How did you like Harry, what did you think of him,
Alan?' Olive is questioning me and I wish she could
understand all I am saying but she looks worried because I
am shaking my head. Olive is trying to find out why I don't
like Harry by asking me lots of questions to which I can reply
'yes' or 'no', but it's mother who finally asks the important
thing.
    'Is it because Harry asked Olive things which you think he
should have asked you?'
    When I indicate 'yes' by nodding my head, Olive responds
by telling me that Harry will be coming later this evening and
she is going to tell him what I said. I am not too worried about
this as I know I will be in bed when Harry comes and I won't
see him.

34

As I lie in bed I can hear Harry has arrived and after a little while he calls to me upstairs, 'Alan, I'm sorry, cock. I will ask you all the questions next time.'

Saturday evening is the time when the children in our home have their weekly bath. The bath is brought in from the back yard and put in front of the living-room fire. Father fills it with buckets of hot water from the boiler in the kitchen. This is always a happy time and it's the only time in the week when the front door is locked. Tonight Harry has come as he and Olive are going dancing. Olive is still getting ready and while Harry is waiting for her, father is allowing him to bath me. Normally father will not allow us to splash while we are in the bath because we wet the whole living-room floor but I cannot resist splashing Harry. He seems quite proud of his wet shirt when Olive appears.

As they are leaving for the dance Harry is promising to come and wash me in the bath next Saturday.

I have got to know Harry well over the weeks. He and Olive are going to be married but I don't seem to be included in their plans. My younger brother, Tom, is to be a pageboy and my two older brothers groomsmen. John is now married and his wife, Mary, will be matron of honour, but I am to be simply a guest. They say it's my age – I am too young to be a groomsman and too old to be a pageboy. I feel left out and hurt. I feel upset about the wedding and it's difficult to talk about it because the family still don't understand what I say to them.

This frustration and the wedding preparations are making me behave in an awkward way and I don't seem to be able to control myself. I have not a kind word to say to anyone and even my mother's wrath does not calm me down. I feel excluded from a major family event for the first time in my life, or at any rate I am more aware of being left out of this event. I am sure that the family have done things without me before but now, at the age of ten, I need to be certain of my place in the family.

Aunty Elsie is going to help me with my eating at the wedding reception and that is something to look forward to. Afterwards she is going to try and teach me to dance.

35

Mother is buying me a new suit for the wedding and I will have my first pair of long trousers. It is a blue suit with a grey check and Harry says he will buy me a tie just like his for me to wear at the wedding.

My sister looks beautiful as a bride. She is wearing a long white dress with a turquoise veil. The veil is very long, longer than the dress and mother says it looks really nice. Olive wanted a white veil but this is the only long one that mother could buy.

Aunty Elsie taught me a barn dance earlier in the evening and now Olive is asking the band to play another so that she can dance with me before she goes away on her honeymoon with Harry. As we are dancing I am not sure why my sister is crying. Is it because she has just got married or is it because I am able to dance with her?

It is taking a long time to overcome the resentment created by feeling excluded from the wedding. I think father realizes how I feel and to help me to overcome this he has assigned me two jobs in the bakehouse. I have to sweep the floor every day and clean the hotplates once a week. The hotplates are almost sacred and every member of the family has asked sometime if they might clean them, but father has always preferred to clean them himself. Now I have been given the job. How important I feel. The hotplates are large, about five feet by three and there are two of them. They have to be sprinkled with sand and rubbed with a big heavy stone until every trace of grease has disappeared; then the sand is swept off them and they have to be washed. Father has a very high standard for them and does not like to see a spot of dirt left. It takes him ten minutes to clean both hotplates. I spend two hours on them, but I don't mind. I am proud of my work and feel good when father praises me.

We now have swimming lessons each week, with the school. I was afraid of the water at first and even now, after about six months, I don't like it. I have not made any progress in swimming and don't really want to go but I cannot be left behind on my own in school. Nor will my teacher allow me to sit and watch. Harry is a good swimmer and has offered to take me to the baths each Saturday morning and try to teach me. He is so patient and makes it almost enjoyable but I just cannot keep afloat. Whenever Harry lets go of me, my hips twist in the water and I panic.

The time arrives when I have to take my eleven-plus examination. All the other children write with pen and ink but I am still writing in pencil and using two hands. I have felt confident about this exam and even boasted to the family about my chances, until now when I realize just how slowly I write. I was able to finish only half of the paper in the time allocated, so I failed. This has made me feel miserable and embarrassed and I feel even worse when I think of the lies I told my family. Even after the exam I could not bring myself to tell the truth and all my family think I must have passed my eleven-plus because I boasted that I thought I'd done well. I'm afraid they are not going to feel sympathetic when they find out how badly I fared.

Around this time I also developed trouble with my eyes. I did not learn eye-control through games because I so seldom played them, and when muscular problems became severe I found that I could not control the opening and closing mechanisms of the eye. Sometimes I would have to prise them open with my fingers. There was nothing wrong with my sight, just with my ability to flex the muscles round the eyes. When this was noticed, Dr Mack gave me some pills, but these made me more floppy and shaky than ever. I almost accepted this – certainly I know I didn't see Dr Mack until the family had noticed the trouble. I got over it, probably because when I went to secondary school I had to keep alert and was desperate to appear as normal as possible. In retrospect it seems like another example of how I was forced to find the willpower and control to make social life, or life outside my family, bearable.

3

My secondary-school building is like my junior school except that it has two storeys. It has the same type of corridor which stretches its full length. From one side you can look out over a quadrangle and see the junior school. On the other side of the corridor are windows, from floor to ceiling, which allows you to see into each classroom. People seem to be interested in watching me write as I sit at a desk by the corridor window. What an oddity I must be – they have never seen anyone using two hands to write before. I have been used to having the same teacher for all classes in my junior school, but now we have a different teacher every hour. No one has spoken to me yet and I feel terribly nervous, as I don't know many of the children. Each teacher who comes into the room stands and watches me work. I don't know if they have been made aware of my problems. By now I have begun to be dimly aware of how destructively self-conscious I am. I used to laugh or cry at all the wrong moments.

At breaktime I have to find my way into the playground and I am amazed at the number of other children walking along the corridor. As all of us have to go down the same staircase to get outside and to the toilets I am frightened to go down with them in case I fall in the crowd. I feel rather shaky and alone because of all the newness and strangeness. I wait until most of the children have descended and then go down carefully holding on to the wall. This makes some of the children laugh. Through the corridor windows they have already seen me writing and they begin to ask me questions. They want to know why I come down the stairs so slowly and why I write the way I do. I am trying to explain to them but they think my talking is hilarious. As I enter the playground more children are asking about my writing and they too find the way I speak funny. It is as much as I can do to stop myself crying. Finally playtime ends and everyone has to go back into school. Again I have not the confidence to climb the stairs with the crowd so I decide to visit the toilet and hope that the stairs will be quieter when I have finished.

In the toilets I meet a boy who has seen me in my classroom and he asks me why I write like that. I try to explain but receive a smack round the head and I am told that in future I will speak properly when I speak to him. I feel like running home to mother, but a teacher appears to hurry us up. As I am climbing the stairs feeling very hurt and sorry for myself I am told to make haste by the teacher. Of course I am late for class and have to explain why.

This is difficult as I am also fighting back tears while I try to talk. Obviously the teacher can't tell what I say and simply pats my head. I feel embarrassed and lost. I wish people could hear the words I speak as I hear them; they are so clear to me.

On my way home from school for lunch I meet Norman, an old friend from junior school. He is also attending the secondary school for the first time today and he chats to me all the way home. I try to explain how I feel. Although he cannot understand much of what I am saying he gets the word 'stairs' and by a process of my nodding and shaking my head to various questions he understands one of my problems. He arranges to be at the staircase whenever possible to help me up and down.

Norman became friendly with me during our last year in junior school when he was having difficulty in memorizing his tables. I knew mine very well and as the other children were rather cruel to Norman, he asked if I would help him. As I spent my playtimes watching the others rather than joining in their games, I welcomed the activity of hearing Norman's tables. I used to try and correct him as he recited to me; although he had difficulty in understanding me, I may have helped him to learn, as I stopped him each time he went wrong. He became friendly to me in school and taught me to

39

kick a ball. I used to fall on my backside each time I lifted a leg but Norman was patient. He was the first friend I ever had in school and I used to think about him all the time; he was very special to me. He had lots of other friends and they used to tease him about being friendly with me. I did not like it when he played games with them rather than being with me. I would have liked to join in their games but they were too rough and my brother wasn't around to help me. Maybe when some of the children in my new school see how clever I am they will be friends with me like Norman was.

I don't really feel like going to school after lunch but mother would never allow me to stay at home and Norman has called for me so that we can walk to school together. As we get to school we are met by a group of children who saw me at breaktime this morning and they are asking questions and are laughing at my efforts to answer. Mercifully the bell sounds for afternoon school. I have decided not to sit near the window as I did this morning. I sit on the opposite side of the room but there is a rumpus as the boy who this morning sat in the seat I have chosen wants the same seat again and I have to return to my original desk. I try to stay in the classroom during afternoon break but this is not allowed, so I lock myself in a toilet until it is time to return to class.

There is a group of children waiting for me at the close of school and they too find the way I speak rather amusing. The journey home has never seemed so long. I am frightened of falling as I am jostled by the crowd. I am so glad to see mother and home seems like a sanctuary. I try to explain to mother what has happened during the day and how miserable I feel but she does not understand half of what I am saying and dismisses my tears by saying that I will eventually make friends.

I cannot go to sleep when I go to bed and I lay scheming as to what I will do tomorrow. I am going to set out as if I am going to school, but make a detour so as to miss all the other children and spend the day in the park. If I don't come home for lunch at the correct time mother will know what I have done, but I know where there is a clock. My plan works very well. I have arrived home for lunch at the right time and feel relieved that I have not been found out. Mother is asking me how school has been this morning. As I nod in reply a letter is thrust at me and as I am reading it I sense mother's anger. The letter is from the headmaster telling mother of my absence from school, making sure that she knew I wasn't there. Someone delivered the letter before lunch. Of course the headmaster knows my parents well through my older brothers and sister, who all went to his school.

The headmaster is waiting for mother and me as we arrive at school after lunch. He takes us to his study, where he asks me where I have been all morning and why.

The study is quiet and the head looks stern and he will not allow mother to answer for me. I have to tell him everything and he takes great pains to understand what I am trying to say. Although I have to repeat my words many times, I can't remember anyone listening to me and wanting to understand me like this man does. He does not seem to care how many times I repeat things to him, he makes me feel that he is interested and has time for me. He summarizes what I have said to make sure that he has understood it correctly and then tells me that the teaching staff are all aware of my problems and all they expect is that I do the best I can. The head's concern now is that I have got behind in the tests we are having this week, which are to find out what stream we should go in. He thinks I will need more time for them than the other children because yesterday I did not complete very much of the papers we were given. He is inviting me to work at a desk in his room until I have completed all the tests, so that I will be placed in the correct stream. He is also telling me to go to him with any problems I may have in the future. As the afternoon is now almost finished I am allowed to go home with my mother.

I think I am lucky to have a headmaster who recognizes that while I might write slowly and with great difficulty, that does not necessarily mean that the papers and tests themselves are too hard for me.

As I work in the head's room during the next three weeks finishing the tests, I am introduced to all the teachers and develop a relationship with the headmaster. There are times

41

at break and when I am walking home that I am harangued by groups of children, but they do me no physical harm and I can bear their harassment because the head discusses it with me. He does not want to make a public announcement about my being in the school; he thinks that might attract even more attention to me and that if I can ignore the comments and refuse to be hurt by them, the bullies will lose interest.

Now that I have completed all the tests I can be placed with a class. It is much better now that I am always with the same group of children and know the teachers who take us for each subject. I am tolerated by the other children in my form and as they get to know me better they understand more of what I say.

At the end of the autumn term the school has a competition which each form must enter. Each class has to produce a play and perform it in front of the whole school. I am certainly not equipped to participate in dramatics and I am wondering what I will be asked to do. I am hoping that I will be left out, but the headmaster has other ideas and insists that I am stage manager for my form. For the first time I have been given responsibility and the staff really involve me.

In my second year I have an art teacher who has an unusual voice. I can't say he has a speech impediment but his voice is nasal and thick and he also has one arm which he cannot straighten. He has difficulty using the hand of that arm. I have never been a success at art and hide away all my work. If I can, I throw it in the wastebin before anyone can see it. But this teacher encourages me and shows a book to the class. It contains pictures by a famous artist and the teacher is asking whose paintings they look like. The other children seem to see a similarity between my work and the pictures in the book. The painting I have today is of a clown and I allow the teacher to pin it up on the wall. It is the very first time any of my work has been displayed. Very slowly people seem to be accepting me as I am and recognize that although I do not have their abilities, I might have others of my own. Knitting is one: I learned it from Mammy Brogden, and though others call it cissy, I enjoy it. Father always wears my scarf, holes and all.

42

Try as I may I still cannot swim. I have lessons at school and Harry still takes me swimming each Saturday morning but I cannot control the rolling of my hips in the water. I have been unable to make any progress.

As the drama competition comes round for the second time I am sent for by the headmaster who suggests that I can write a play for my class to perform. I don't really feel that I can do this but the headmaster is persuasive, so I have a try.

I have written a play and called it *The Rose-coloured Spectacles*. It is a sort of fairy tale about a bad-tempered princess who is disliked by all her subjects and family; she is given a pair of rose-coloured spectacles which make her good-tempered and likeable, she meets her Prince Charming, marries him and lives happily ever after. The headmaster edited it for me and I noticed the number of corrections he made to the script. I was amazed that he never commented on any mistake but instead gave a lot of praise for the idea behind the script. My form produce it on stage and it is well received by the audience. But I am embarrassed when at the end of the play I am introduced as the author and there are a few laughs from the audience. However, I think I became more generally accepted at school through writing this play.

There are times, though, when life is difficult and I am still ridiculed, and then I go through hell. The teachers stand back and allow me to fight my own battles because they think the label 'teacher's pet' might make matters worse. The school caretaker is a great ally and will often come to my rescue. He never says a word but his presence is enough to send my tormentors running. Many a time my coat will be thrown high over the bars in the cloakroom or up a tree in the school playground where it is impossible for me to get it down. On these occasions I am always relieved to see the caretaker appear to retrieve my coat when everyone has miraculously disappeared. It is as though he does not want anyone to see him helping me.

When my form do physical training I usually join in and try to play as the others do, but now we have a new teacher who asks me to sit and watch. I hate this and feel different from

43

the rest. Fortunately the headmaster sees me watching the others and wants to know why. Obviously he has a word with the teacher and I am allowed to join in, although I don't think I am popular with the physical-training teacher as a result. But I am still so scared of other children.

I have an awkward streak and I want to try and feed myself. Mother says I am not ready for this. I make too much mess and take too long. However, my tantrums are such that she has to allow me to have my own way. Mother is constantly telling me not to suck my food but to chew it.

We have a large table in the centre of the living room which is used by everyone for all sorts of activities. We have the parlour too, but that is seldom heated and is kept for when we have visitors. The living room is always a centre of activity and the table is invariably being used for something or other. My father and I have the same old argument time after time. Each evening I practise my writing, using one hand, and my father counts the money he has taken that day, both of us using the table at the same time. In order to steady my hand while I am writing, I put a lot of pressure on my pencil and the table shakes as I write. Father's piles of coins are knocked over; he has to count them again and gets annoyed. After this has happened one evening we all sit down to our meal. As often happens, my arm – the one used for feeding myself – goes into a spasm. It sends the contents of my spoon across the table and they hit father in the face. He accepts this as an accident, but mother is not sure that I have not done it to get my own back for the quarrel father and I had earlier!

Gradually my writing is improving and I can write for short periods using one hand. I have made friends in school and although they don't always understand my words I am able to communicate with them by using speech and gesture. I have one special friend who also has a handicap. There is something wrong with her glands and she is terribly fat. Many of the children give her a bad time and as she too is often laughed at, we find we have many difficulties in common. My friend is called Eileen. We are not included in the other children's activities away from school and we feel

44

that others tend to get more pleasure out of life than we do. I have a pet mongrel, and I love him but know there should be something better. So Eileen and I make a plan.

My mother almost has a heart attack when I ask if I might go to the cinema alone. Until now I have always gone with one of my brothers. My going alone is a case for family discussion and for a start everyone wonders why I want to go. They are also concerned about how I will cope with a crowded bus and the busy town centre. I am not very steady on my feet and I am easily knocked over. Sometimes if I fall I still cannot get up by myself. Actually, I have no intention of going on my own. I have arranged to go with Eileen, but I am not going to tell my family that, as they would not understand and probably would not approve either.

My awkwardness and tantrums win the day as usual and I have been given permission to go into town next Saturday.

The great day has arrived. I get on the bus at the stop at the bottom of the street and look towards the next stop where Eileen should be waiting. The bus is full and I am afraid that Eileen will not be able to get on. Luckily she does. We have to stand all the way into town but I am quite safe as there is a pole to hang on to.

The town is very busy and I am a little scared. I do not want to hold on to Eileen's arm but neither do I like to be in a crowd when people are rushing about with shopping bags. However, Eileen and I have no trouble in getting to the cinema and I feel quite grown-up as I pay for two tickets from the money I have saved from the jobs I do for father in the bakehouse.

When we get inside the cinema it is dark. Always before, one of my brothers has taken my arm as we looked for a seat but today I am not with a familiar guide. I did not expect to react to the darkness as I have. My balance has gone, I feel very frightened and the only thing I can do is drop to my knees and crawl. I feel embarrassed but Eileen says I worry too much and as it is a new experience what did I expect?

We both enjoy the film although my mind is leaping ahead and wondering if the lights will be on at the end. I do not fancy crawling out. I felt undignified enough crawling into darkness but the thought of crawling from the cinema is even worse. I need not have worried because when the lights do come on I am able to walk out normally.

Mother is asking all about my visit to the cinema and wants to know if I met anyone I knew. Of course I answer with an emphatic 'no', but something in mother's smile makes me feel uneasy.... As I lie in bed later, Joe is telling me that he was assigned to follow me this afternoon to make sure no harm came to me and he saw me with Eileen. He is giving me a lot of stick about it as though I was involved in a big love affair. Next, father and mother are pulling my leg as I eat breakfast. I am trying desperately to explain about Eileen but they only understand what they want to. Despite all the ribbing, the experience of going into town alone has given me confidence. Having had this experience I would like to learn to dance with Eileen. There are a number of church halls around my home which have dances each Saturday evening, mostly attended by old women and children. Eileen and I think it might be fun to go along and teach ourselves to dance. At first mother will not hear of it. She says that I am too young at fourteen to be out dancing on Saturday evenings. However, Eileen's mother is going with us, so I am eventually allowed to go. Soon it becomes the usual practice for Eileen and me to go dancing every Saturday, although her mother does not often come with us. We get along very well together but I never have anything to eat or drink as it would be too embarrassing in public. I am conscious that I do not chew my food. Mother is always on at me not to suck, but I cannot chew. I am often sick after I have eaten and the doctor says it is because I bolt my food and I should chew it more. I know what he means. I watch my family eat but when I try to chew like they do I find I can only suck. Still, I make less mess when I eat than I used to, so I must be improving.

Eileen and I often laugh at and discuss the attitudes of people towards us at these evenings. They talk to us as though we were five-year-olds, they put on my coat and do up my buttons, and they help us down the steps; old women have even been known to give up their seats to us. We have decided that the only way to stop this kind of thing is for us to

46

act more like normal fourteen-year-olds. We have decided to leave the dance early and wait in the cloakroom ready to hold the coats for the older women; we are going to help them down the steps and if they speak patronizingly, we are going to admire something about them. This is the night when we are to begin our new tactics and as I usually speak only to my family and a very few friends, I feel dreadfully nervous. Here it comes, a stroke on the cheek.

'Aye, he's a grand lad. Have you brought your little girlfriend for a dance? Aren't they lovely?' This is addressed half to Eileen and me and half to the company around us.

I reply, 'I do like your dress.'

Now the woman is asking those around her in a mystified voice, 'Did he try and talk to me?' Then Eileen is addressed. 'What's he saying, what's he saying? He did talk to me, didn't he?'

I want to run and hide for now this woman is announcing to those within earshot, 'Aye, isn't he lovely, he tried to talk to me,' as though a miracle was happening. The opening notes of another dance allow Eileen and me to escape but I feel depressed, even though Eileen is trying to talk me out of my gloom.

Eileen and I suffer great indignities from many people who misunderstand our friendship. They cannot understand that Eileen and I have joined forces because it is an easy way out for us. We both feel a barrier between ourselves and normal people, and we find a companionship in each other's company that is a substitute for the loneliness we know we both would suffer if we had not befriended each other. We are brutally realistic and tell each other frequently that we would not be such friends if it were not for our handicaps.

Many people of our age group have special relationships with one or several friends and discuss all kinds of problems which are part of the transition from childhood to adulthood. Many of these relationships hold something special, something that gives them strength and confidence, and, not least, a social life. Although Eileen and I have an excellent relationship an element is missing, something which I cannot put a name to but which is necessary to every close

47

relationship. I am lonely and would like to be more popular and to have more friends. Although I welcome Eileen's friendship I am still frustrated when I fail to make friends with others. Fortunately I have a close relationship with my brothers and this is some compensation for the lack of outside friends. I envy the ease with which others seem to form groups. It seems to be such a difficult thing to do. It is not just a question of communication; I feel there are other elements involved. I wonder what skills I have not developed during my early isolation. I feel that others have an advantage over me in as much as they began to make friends at an early age while I was stuck in the house with my mother, unable to walk. I also think of the years when I had to go to the girls' playground in school rather than the boys' playground, and wonder whether this was good for me. I don't know whether I would have learned more about how to make friends in the boys' playground, but I seem to be trying to figure out in my own mind how I can make friends and why I feel so awkward whenever I have the opportunity of integrating and getting to know more people. I have discussed this problem with my mother who says that there are a great many people who find it hard to make friends, but this is of no solace to me. Eileen has the same problem and like me cannot understand why, or find a solution.

At last I feel I may have found a relationship which may be of help to me. John, my eldest brother, has returned from military service and has a baby boy. I spend a great deal of time with this family and my nephew gives me something which is intangible and undefinable but which I know I have never felt before. He always welcomes me and seems to like having me around. He is actually demanding my attention and does not seem to tire of me. I love the feeling this gives me. My brother and his wife are friendly and share much of their life with me. My sister-in-law has a hearing problem and has been taught to lip-read, so she can tell what I say easily. These splendid people are my constant companions and offer me a relationship which is different from the others I have. When I speak to my sister-in-law I feel like I've been freed from a prison and from a darkness. I know she must get fed up with me because I talk to her non-stop. It is such a relief to speak to someone and be understood 100 per cent. Not only that, but having a two-way conversation is something which is new to me and it releases a lot of my frustration. There are times when my brother is cross because I want to monopolize his wife's time but then he apologizes and says he knows it's hard for me.

John is now working in a garage and has a car. Each Saturday after lunch he calls for me and we go to the seaside or out into the country. On our way back he takes us for fish and chips. I always want to eat them in the car, but John insists that I eat in the restaurant as he thinks I should learn to eat in public. Although I can feed myself I still make a mess on the table and I hate people to stare at me. John says it's all in my mind and people don't stare, and if they do I should stare back because I am good enough to be stared at.

Obviously John needs time with his wife and family without me around and I am asked not to visit him on Sundays. After all, I'm there almost every other day. I sometimes go straight from school and if his wife is at our house I offer to push the pram up the big hill to their home so that I can be with them for a little while.

By now my sister has also had a little boy and I am invited to tea with the family each Sunday. They don't have a car so we go for walks or play Monopoly and my sister and I end up giggling together. Harry has always been patient with me and tries to understand my speech. He also helps me to write using only one hand and tells me I must try to form the letters more slowly and then my handwriting will improve. They have just bought their home and are decorating it. They hope to make a garden in the back yard by taking up some of the paving stones. I would like to help and I offer to make the garden for them but Olive says the stones are too heavy and I may hurt myself. Harry thinks I should try and do what I can, so here I am breaking up paving stones and moving them to the bottom of the yard. As my sister said, they are heavy, but I am sure I can manage if I take my time. The garden is finished and Harry says my sister is really proud of it, more so than she would have been if he had done it.

The time is approaching when I shall have to leave school and there is much speculation about what I am going to do. Many people have ideas about what they think I should do and I am feeling anxious. The majority of the children at school have got work to go to. Even Eileen has got a job as a clerk in the office of a coal merchant in Mincing Lane. Joe is a great consolation to me. He thinks we should plan what I could do if I don't get a job straight from school and he has outlined all the jobs I could do in the bakehouse to help father. Father would prefer me to find work elsewhere; he thinks I will never ever be able to take over the bakehouse completely and that if I start working for him the authorities may not help me to find work and I might be worse off in the long run.

There is a sweetshop for sale near our house and father is proposing to buy it for me so that I might make a living through it. He is prepared to mortgage the house and the bakehouse to buy it and grandmother is also willing to lend some money, but I don't want the shop. People cannot tell what I say and that would be a distinct disadvantage for a shopkeeper! Mother is also against the idea because she is concerned about all the debt we would incur in buying the shop. My sister-in-law has discussed it with me and has told father how I feel. He is keen to listen and when he fully understands my viewpoint he agrees with me. So the idea of the shop is out.

I am now the only one in my year at school without a job. I have seen many people about work but they are all discouraging. I went for a medical because I have to register as a disabled person and the doctor who saw me said that I was not really fit or capable for work and when I am eighteen I will receive an allowance of some kind for my support. I feel very depressed and cry myself to sleep each night. Joe comforts me when he hears my sobs and tries to cheer me. He is more hopeful than I am that a job will come along. He has been called into the army and I realize that this will never happen to me. I also start to wonder whether I shall ever be married or even have a girlfriend. It's bad enough being the way I am, but not having a job makes things worse ... I

50

cannot see me being of any worth to anyone. Who would want to associate with me, my abilities are so limited? I feel so miserable and ill that mother insists that I stay in bed and the doctor is called in.

I have been in bed for about two weeks and the doctor says I can get up tomorrow. Mother is being very mischievous, and says she has a surprise for me but won't tell me what it is until she hears me laugh again. It must be something nice for she has a gleam in her eye.

I have to be carried downstairs as I have grown so weak that I cannot walk and this worries me, but the doctor says I will be all right in a few days. He tells me I have lain in bed for too long and that the medicine he gave me has made my limbs too relaxed. I can't feed myself either but mother says I will be able to again in a little while. I feel sad and desperately wish I could get work, but now I can't walk any more my chances are even worse. I wonder if it's worth making the effort to try to walk or feed myself again. My family, not surprisingly, are fed up with me and say it's time I pulled myself together and got better. Father is threatening not to carry me down the stairs if I do not try to walk and mother says she will not feed me anymore, I have to feed myself. I haven't eaten for two days and mother and father are arguing because father wants to feed me but mother says if I am hungry I will feed myself. Mother is insistent and at last I try. I think there is more food down the front of me and on the table than I have managed to get into my mouth, but mother is pleased and has taken me on her lap to feed me my pudding. If I try to walk to the front door and back mother says she will tell me her secret. I have never wobbled so much in my life as I do when I walk down the lobby; I make it to the front door but I can't get back because my legs won't go. Mother has to carry me back. I wonder if she will still tell me her secret?

My father arrives home from work as mother and I reach the top of the lobby. He wants to know why mother is carrying me, and mother is telling him what has happened. As she sits me in a chair she is telling father that she has been to visit a man whom she used to know many years ago when she worked in the cotton mill. He is the cashier at a mill near to us and he has said that if I can walk again he will get me a job as a warehouse boy. This is mother's surprise. I can't believe it. Father wants to know when this happened. Mother says some time ago but she wanted to be sure that I was going to recover before she told me, as she thought it would have affected me badly if I knew I had a job but could never get to it. Now she is sure that I will get better. If only mother had told me before! I feel better already. The promise of a job is all I need. I can feel determination return. I realize that my illness has been largely psychological.

The doctor is pessimistic. He agrees that my illness could have happened because I could not see any hope for my future, but he also says that according to medical facts I should not be able to walk at all and that maybe my walking days are over. But he was wrong before and I know I shall walk again. Walking does not hurt me but my legs feel heavy and dragging. Still, if I use the bakehouse each day to practise, I know I will get better. After all, in the past, hasn't the doctor said I would improve? I wonder if he is doubting this now. I think it is about time that I knew what was really wrong with me but mother says she does not know and she does not really want to know as she has every confidence in the doctor: he has said I will grow out of it and even I must admit that I have made physical progress. When I ask the doctor what has been wrong with me all my life he is evasive and tells me that too much knowledge would be bad for me.

One of my teachers has come to visit me in my home and he is offering to arrange for some of the boys in my year to push me to school in a wheelchair, but I refuse. I have been away from school for five weeks and I would like to get back, but I would prefer it if two boys were to come and help me walk to school. No wheelchair, I'm adamant. It's all arranged, although the doctor doesn't think I ought to go back to school. I have two friends coming for me on Monday morning and I shall walk to school between them and lean on them if necessary. I have learned to ignore the doctor. It is no use discussing my plans with too many people. They only understand a little of what I say and I feel more frustrated about this than previously. I still can't understand why people can't hear the words I speak the way they sound in my head.

I made it to school this morning and everyone seems pleased to see me. I'm glad to be back.

It's a little difficult to walk home at lunchtime but I manage with the help of my two friends. Mother is insisting that I go to bed and rest this afternoon and is going to see the headmaster to arrange for me to go to school for the morning session only until I get stronger.

I still have real difficulty in eating. Around this time I go through a period of disappearing at mealtimes to visit an elderly neighbour, Mrs Heap. She told mother that I managed to eat perfectly well, and although mother was embarrassed that I had invited myself to tea, she was interested to hear that, with a spoon and a newspaper under my chair, I was able to eat at my own pace. As a result, mother agreed to bend the rules at home, and let me have a cooked evening meal rather than sandwiches, which I found difficult, with the others. I ate more and became stronger.

It is four weeks to the day before I start work and I have to go and meet the manager of the mill. It's very noisy and I am alarmed at all the machinery but I am keen to work and the manager is prepared to employ me.

I like the idea of starting work more and more and it's comforting to know that I have an aunt and uncle who work at the same mill. Eileen's mother does too.

My walking has improved and I feel as well as I did before I became ill. The doctor insists that from now on I visit him once a week whether I'm sick or not, and so the Wednesday evening visits begin. I need to be fit to start work and because I'm afraid of getting overtired I go to bed at 7.30 each evening. This makes my family laugh but I am not taking any chances. I don't want anything to stop me from starting my job after the New Year's holiday.

4

The mill is hot, dusty and noisy and it is going to take me some while to get used to it. The people who work here are jolly and make me feel welcome. I am wearing my first pair of bib-and-brace overalls, which help me to feel like a real workman. It is peculiar to think that I am no longer a schoolboy.

My job in the warehouse is to wrap and stack bales of material after they have been inspected and folded. Often the bales are so heavy and the stacks so high that I just cannot manage them, I'm too weak. Joe the bundler is always close at hand and will come and stack for me when he sees me struggling. He sometimes takes the mickey out of me but it's all in fun.

Another aspect of my work is to 'dress' material which has a repairable fault. I spend many hours with a toothbrush scrubbing at specks of black oil which have got into a roll of material as it is being woven. This is a boring job but when such faults happen, the weaver whose loom the cloth came off is fined and the money is given to me.

No matter what I am doing my first priority is to answer the call of the cut-lookers, who are the people responsible for the state of the material. The cut-looker will send for a weaver to discuss any fault found in their weaving. At times these discussions get heated and are interesting to overhear, to put it mildly. The cut-lookers hardly ever use four-letter words to the weavers but some of the weavers use language which ought to be censored. I am the one who goes into the weaving shed to tell weavers they are wanted in the warehouse and so my appearance there is always viewed with apprehension. The weavers are not always polite to me and I sometimes wonder if they think it's my fault that there is something wrong with their weaving. The noise in the mill makes it impossible to hear exactly what people are saying but quite often when I go to call a weaver to the warehouse I am left in no doubt as to what is being said; the facial expressions and gesticulations of some of the weavers turn the air blue around their heads!

Sometimes the fault in the weaving is caused through the neglect of the tacklers, who are responsible for the mechanics of the looms. I was told on my first day of work, if I was ever sent to summon a tackler to the warehouse to do it from afar and then run for cover. This piece of advice is exceptionally sound because the tacklers in general are the most bad-tempered and foul-mouthed group of people I have ever met.

Most of the people I have met in the mill have been friendly and helpful and have treated me just like they do the other warehouse boys. Reference is never made to my handicap, but my ear is clipped whenever my behaviour is unacceptable.

In the weaving shed there is a terribly narrow alley, that is, a space between two rows of looms, where I have to walk to tell some of the weavers that they are wanted in the warehouse. I am afraid when I have to walk down this alley because there is only about twelve inches' gap and on each side there is machinery and picking sticks, which swing out from each side of the loom and send the shuttle across the warp. They move rhythmically and have a strong force behind them. Many of the weavers feel I should not be allowed to enter the weaving shed let alone walk down this treacherous alley, because of my unsteady gait. These weavers have sent a deputation to the management saying that they fear for my safety and are concerned that I might fall into the machinery.

It has been decided, then, that I will have a new role at the mill. Instead of doing the normal job of a warehouse boy I will dress material and help around the warehouse and do any shopping for employees but I am not allowed in the

55

weaving shed. I feel embarrassed about this but Raymond and Arthur, the other warehouse lads, are enthusiastic and encouraging. They are going to collect orders from the weaving shed each morning and deliver the shopping as I get it. They think that I should continue to bale and stack the cloth as this activity may help develop my muscles.

Through my shopping I make quite a bit of money each week in tips, which I share with Raymond and Arthur.

I am self-conscious about my speech and never make conversation. If other people speak to me I nod or smile but I try not to talk to anyone outside my family. Tea breaks are an embarrassment to me as I cannot drink in the mill without spillages. This is because I need to be sitting on the right height of chair at the right height of table and there are no convenient chairs or tables at the mill. I make an awful mess each time that I have a drink. The other lads are good-hearted and will not allow me to sit on my own at breaktimes. They try to include me in their conversation and I wish they would not. I find it frustrating as I have to repeat myself over and over again. I suppose they think it would be bad-mannered to leave me on my own; I would prefer it that way but they refuse to accept my preference for solitude.

The warehouse lads are often invited to other mill departments for tea breaks. I am included in these invitations but can never bring myself to go. I get frightened at the thought of being in strange company, especially that of men. I feel very self-conscious and inferior, so much so that I will not use the toilets at the mill. There is always a group of men in there smoking and I am afraid if I go in they might talk to me and I would have to answer them.

Frustration eats away inside me all the time because of my speech. I have even tried to discuss it with the doctor but he cannot help. Dr Mack says I should be thankful for what I am because I could have had a much worse handicap. My sister-in-law understands how I feel about not being able to join in conversations because of her hearing difficulties, but even she can only sympathize and has no solution to offer.

It is helpful, all the same, to talk with Dr Mack each Wednesday afternoon. I am developing a personal relationship with him and although he can offer no remedies, he does help me to see how other people might regard me.

Many of the young people at the mill are going to take a course in textiles at the local technical college. I am invited to go by two work-mates, Raymond and Arthur, but I do not have the confidence to join them as I think I might be required to do a lot of note-taking and my writing is so slow. I also guess that I will have to meet new people and this I hate because of my speech. Whenever I meet someone new I am always faced with the same old question of what I should do. If I don't speak to them I offend them and they think I am stuck up. If I do speak to them they respond in one of four ways: they look at me in horror and think that I am mad; they shout at me, thinking my impeded speech means I am also deaf; they hear the sound of my voice and begin to ask those around me questions which should be asked of me; or they speak to me as they would to a baby or a beloved family pet. No one ever responds to me as they would to a normal person and I feel that if I went to these evening classes I would suffer even more frustration, even though I know meeting new people might be good for me.

I often feel like screaming when I am with others because I would like to contribute to their discussions and most of all I would like people to know that behind this façade of a severe speech impediment and shaky, wobbly limbs there is a real person, an individual with hopes, fears, needs, feelings and thoughts all of which are suppressed and cannot be expressed because I cannot convey much sense to any listener. Dr Mack thinks I should try to explain the way I feel to the two other warehouse lads.

My conversation is being approached by Raymond and Arthur rather like the daily crossword puzzle, with every clue from my speech being studied earnestly and every correct answer considered a triumph.

'It's something about evening classes.'
'You don't want to go?'
'Oh, you do want to go?'
On and on it goes until they have got an impression of what I am trying to say without fully understanding my remarks.

They are both offering to help me if I will go along with them. I can always drop out if it is too embarrassing.

We have settled down on our textile course and have devised a system whereby Raymond and Arthur take all the notes and copy them for me and I share the answers to our homework with them.

There are lots of laughs between us as we progress with our course. I don't think we are taking our studies seriously enough and we often do stupid things. I think I enjoy being one of the lads as much as anything else.

In our present session we have been given the task of stripping down a jacquard loom, which is a complicated procedure. This kind of loom is for weaving fancy brocades. It is not our night. The mechanisms of the jacquard are about nine feet from the ground and I am not steady standing on the floor let alone on a ladder. Raymond and Arthur are flummoxed and are asking me if I know what to do. Well, I do, but I cannot clearly explain it, let alone do it. I am afraid that I will fall if I climb up and I doubt if I have the required dexterity to carry out the task. We make very slow progress. At the end of the session our loom is still in pieces, while all the other groups have completed theirs. The head of the textile department is annoyed and is ordering us to return to college on Saturday morning to put the loom back together again. I feel guilty because of my lack of physical contribution. I have just been standing all evening shouting instructions. Raymond and Arthur could not care less and are laughing about the situation; they will not hear of my not coming with them on Saturday morning. I feel they may get on faster and better without me but they think quite differently, saying they will never get the loom back together if I am not there to tell them how it is done.

What fun we are having. There is no one else in the textile department. Each time I shout an instruction and it is not understood I get the giggles, which seem to be infectious. It has taken us four hours to put the loom together. It should have taken one. I wonder at my success in forming this relationship with them. It has not always been an easy relationship but they have corrected many of my immature and unacceptable traits. When I began at the mill I really had no idea of how to be part of any social conversation. Whenever anybody spoke to me I used to stand there with my mind vacant and had no contribution or reply to make, unless of course the communication warranted a yes or no answer. Raymond and Arthur would tell me how I could have replied to leg-pulls, conversations and jokes. They literally taught me the skills of social verbal interchange. It was as though they understood my problem without anyone having explained it to them. Of course my responses were not very well understood, but I learned much which I could store for future use. I sometimes think they may have accidentally taught me many things which I would normally have learned during the formation of relationships in early childhood. I do not think they knew that they were teaching me, but nevertheless they have added to my maturity. I have now experienced adult friendship as well as having a stable relationship with my family; both have been important and have helped me to understand and to learn.

On reflection, all the weavers have contributed much to my social training. Having formed few relationships during my early life I did not understand or know how to handle the acceptance that the weavers showed to me. I would take advantage of these relationships and pull the weavers' hair or untie their aprons and be very childish and cheeky. The weavers would clip my ear and I soon learned how to behave better with people. I doubt if any of them were aware of what they were teaching me.

Mother is spending more and more time at my grand-mother's home. She is helping to nurse her because her health is failing. This is a worrying time as grandmother has been so dear to me and I know that she is probably going to die.

I have come home from work this evening to an empty house and when my father enters after me I can tell by his eyes and his white lips that he has bad news. My heart is thumping in my chest as I look into father's face and read the unspoken announcement.

59

'Is it grandmother? She's dead, isn't she?' Father is nodding his head. 'Grandmother dead,' I repeat to myself. Father looks at me with sorrow.

'Yes, she is dead. Mother was with her at the end. It's all over.'

'Where is mother now?' I ask.

'She has stayed with your aunties. She will be home later.' Father looks as though he is in a trance and I feel rather strange.

'I will go and draw the curtains in the parlour,' I hear myself saying. I walk into the other room in a daze. I look through the window and on to the street where grandmother and I have walked many times but will never walk again.

As I pull the curtains to cover the window my thoughts race about in my head. I can't not have a grandmother. She has always been with me. I can't be without her. How funny life is. Suddenly the tears come and I cry uncontrollably. I feel a dreadful void deep inside me and I also feel confused at my tears. I feel most unsure that a lad of my age should be weeping like this.

My blunt fingernails dig into my clammy palms as I try to control my sobbing and suddenly it seems ironical that a person such as I, a person who is different from most people, should experience something which must be common to many. Maybe my life is more normal than I think. Oh, but how am I going to live without my dear grandmother?

On my return to the living room two hours later, I am greeted by the tear-stained face of my father. I am surprised that father has allowed himself the relief of tears, just as I have. The fact that we have both cried, in separate rooms, means that father is allowing me to grow up by respecting my privacy. On previous occasions when I have been upset I have been showered by consolations.

Father says, 'You will be all right now that you have cried it out of your system.' He has made a pot of tea but I am so upset that I am quite unable to control my shakes and father has to hold my cup while I drink.

60

It is hard for me to come to terms with the finality of death. I have never experienced someone close to me dying before and I cannot accept that I will never see grandmother again. She was my companion when I was quite helpless as a child. She understood me better than anyone. So much comfort has been brought into my life through grandmother. I know that people die all the time but I had somehow thought that because of my handicap death would not deprive me of those people who support and sustain me in life, the people I need most of all.

I am so shocked that for the last few weeks I have needed help with feeding again because my hands shake so much. My family try to console me in various ways but there is a dull pain inside me which will not go away. How can I come to terms with this loss?

This is surely the worst emotional experience I have had in my short life. But I must begin to take up the threads of life again and resign myself to facts: the fact that I too am subject to nature's laws and conditions even though I might be handicapped. My mother, herself upset deeply, can do without my depression.

I have done some deep thinking over the past few weeks. Is there a god? Is death the end or is the promise of another life true? Will I see my grandmother again?

Eventually I am resigned to grandmother's death. I have found a part of myself which has only emerged through the blow. Through grandmother's passing I am more aware of my emotional self, more conscious of my ability to feel. This is the first time that I have been aware of thinking deeply. The fact that I am aware of my mother's feelings and how my grumpy mood adds to her hurt is something new, for up until now I must have been very selfish, too full of myself. I have taken my family's presence, care and attention for granted. Now I'm aware of changes in myself, and, dimly, of the notion of normality. Up until now I have thought that I was entirely handicapped but having thought my way through this period I realize that there is a great deal of normality in me, in my mental processes, my responses and reactions. Dreadful though that period was, it demonstrated to me that in lots of ways I was subject to the emotional laws that apply to everyone.

Although I have made progress with my speech and communication is much easier now in my work, I do wonder if the improvement is simply due to the people I have to work with each day having got used to me. Sometimes I think that I may just have developed a way of communicating in my day-to-day routine the things I need to convey without the need for real language. I am obsessed with speech and feel very shy and withdrawn in most company. It is with strangers, away from work, that I feel the most frustrated.

I often have dreams where I speak nicely. Sometimes in my dreams there are lots of girls and they are all laughing at me as I speak. Then I wake up in tears. I visit the library every Saturday and find books about speaking, anything about speaking. I need to understand how the words which can sound so clear to me come out of my mouth so unintelligibly.

How can I express my thoughts when my words aren't understood? How can I get answers to straightforward, let alone vaguely metaphysical, questions when I can't even voice those questions? How can I get to know myself when I do not know how to formulate the questions which might lead me to the theories and ideas which will help me to understand? People seem to react instinctively to life and living but words are how they understand themselves and think their way through dilemmas. Words express thoughts and expressed thoughts clarify our inner language. What a disadvantage it is both socially and psychologically not to be able to express one's thoughts, even if sometimes only to oneself. I think so far I have concentrated on the clarity of single words rather than the meaning of stringing words together. I have not practised and therefore never developed linguistic thinking. There are concepts in the use of language which I have yet to learn but as I become more aware of my problems, I tune in to what other people are doing with language. I learn more from being involved with people and from listening to them than I do from books. I realize how much training I missed in early life. My speech was never corrected as a child. How could it be, when the sounds I made were unintelligible? And I never even developed the ability to form questions.

My nephews are continually being taught how to pronounce their words and how to structure their language, and as I am so close to them I am learning a great deal. I am discovering with my nephews the things I would have learned incidentally as a child had my speech been normal. In school each child in the class had to read aloud to the rest of the class and a lot of correction took place then, but because my words were never clear the teacher would always bypass me. Even my written work was not corrected by the teacher. Initially it was not readable and when my writing improved there was so little of it and it took such an effort to produce that the teacher simply ticked it – not, no doubt, out of neglect, but out of misguided kindness. Now that I am so behind I wish more brutal efforts had been taken with me.

Many of my problems would have been easier to live with if I could have discussed them fully with someone, but I fear that my conversation is made stilted by the pressures on the listener. My speech is still difficult to understand and long conversations are a big effort for both parties.

I have now become fascinated with language and speech and find reading books on the subject absorbing, *The Golden Voice* by Florence Pope being the most interesting book I have read so far.

Eileen has been going to singing lessons for some years now and she is often asked to sing in concerts and at parties. I sometimes go with her and I don't know where she gets her confidence from. She has an excellent voice and is becoming increasingly popular. I wonder if her music teacher might be able to help me with my speaking. Now that I am earning a wage I could afford to pay.

Miss Nuttall, Eileen's music teacher, is a great help to me. She says she cannot do much because her training is for the normal voice, but she is prepared to do all she can. As well as being Eileen's music teacher she is a friend of Eileen's mother and I think that is why she is bothering to see me at all.

What has been most useful for me is learning how the different sounds are made and attempting to make these sounds by trying to make my vocal organs work the same as those of a normal person. It is proving a success but no one sees the sweat and tears which go into each inch of progress.

Each evening Eileen and I get together and practise making sounds. Eileen produces the sound first and I try to imitate it. When the sound is as pure as the one Eileen made I then produce it again, trying to concentrate and taking special note of what my throat muscles are doing. Eileen keeps a record of the way I can best make each sound. Our notebook says things like: 'cannot make a good "E" without smiling . . . to make a good "A" sound tuck chin into chest . . . when saying "dirty" hold bottom jaw so that the top and bottom teeth line up straight otherwise "dirty" sounds like "thirsty" . . . makes a better "th" sound when head is slightly forward.'

We spend hours each week just practising sounds. I don't know how Eileen bears it. We don't do anything else hour after hour. I do listen to Eileen practising her songs, though; our lives revolve around sounds and singing.

We practise putting these sounds together very carefully to form words. I never realized before how complicated language is. A short word like 'bucket' demands that five sounds are strung together. If one of these sounds is incorrect it can sound like another word. So we practise and practise and practise.

It has been many months since we began this work, but I know that I am improving because of the way people are responding when I speak to them. Many people are commenting on this improvement, which is good for my confidence. My family are understanding my speech much better than they did before, but my main problem is still with strangers.

Not only has my speech improved but suddenly I can now chew. Mother has noticed this too; it is as though learning to use my vocal muscles has loosened my jaw. I no longer need

64

to mash my food to a pulp with my fork before eating it – I can now cut a piece of meat and chew it. I go slowly but nevertheless I can now begin to eat and digest properly.

I have been at work a year and a half now and I know that I am walking much better than I used to. My job is boring; Raymond and Arthur think I should try walking through the weaving shed again to see if I feel able to take up the more interesting duties of a warehouse lad once more. This would give some variety to my life at the mill. The narrow alley still scares me, but as Raymond is guiding me down I feel more confident than I did when I first began to work here.

I approached the manager this morning about resuming the duties of a warehouse lad and to my surprise he said he had noticed how much better I was doing and had wondered if I should return to the job for which I had originally been employed. He mentioned the way I am now able to throw bundles around, which I was unable to do when I started. So I happily return to my duties as a proper warehouse lad.

Raymond and Arthur are forever telling me about their activities away from the mill and invite me to join them, but I don't feel I could cope with their kind of social life. They both drink and they both have girlfriends. I say I think it would be a laugh to see me with a pint of beer in a pub. I would shampoo the carpet with my beer and other people in the pub might be entertained by my struggles. As for girlfriends, I have never kissed a girl in my life. I have to make a conscious effort not to dribble and I don't suppose any girl would like to be kissed by someone like me. Anyway I don't know how to kiss. Raymond and Arthur say one does not need teaching to kiss as it comes naturally.

As Eileen and I are working on our sounds tonight I begin to ask some rather personal questions.

'Eileen, have you ever been kissed?'

'No, Alan. Have you?'

'No, I haven't, but Raymond and Arthur were talking at work today and what they said started me thinking about kissing.'

'What about it?'

'Well, what do you do, what is a kiss, do you suck, do you press your lips together or what?'

'Oh, Alan, you are a twirp. A kiss is a kiss.'

'But what is a kiss?'

'We could go on like this all night; we will find out sooner or later, I'm sure.'

'But, Eileen, we are missing out on so much. Other people of our age have got girlfriends and boyfriends and are out drinking and dancing and enjoying life. We seem to do nothing but work. I don't even know how to kiss a girl.'

'This is a conversation I don't really want to get involved in – surely you have kissed your mother and your sister?'

'That's not like kissing a girl.' At least I knew that much.

'All right, are we going to carry on with this ridiculous conversation or are we going to work?'

We did a little work tonight but Eileen asked if I would walk her home early and I sensed a funny mood upon her as we approached her house.

'I am going in the back way tonight.'

'That is unusual. Why?' I ask.

'Well, mum and dad will be at the front of the house and I thought we might do some practising before you went home.'

'But it's very dark going the back way.'

'Yes, Alan, are you thick as well as daft? I want you to kiss me.'

'Eileen, I did not have this in mind when I asked about kissing earlier.'

'Didn't you? Come on, I dare you to kiss me.'

'But Eileen, what if I dribble on you?'

'Try not to.'

Suddenly our lips are together and I believe what Arthur and Raymond said ... kissing comes naturally.

Eileen and I have been working on my speech for about two years and now that progress has been made we feel dissatisfied and we want more out of life. We want to be more like other people of our age.

We have been dancing for the last three Saturdays and we dance with each other, but I think we would both like to

66

widen our circle of friends. But how can I do so through dancing? I have mastered the steps. I can even dance a quickstep now whereas a few months ago it was too fast for me, so certainly my legs are improving. But my right hand wriggles when I put it on my partner's back and I have to hold my thumb in my fist to control it, which can't be very comfortable for her. Eileen says that I am over-sensitive about my wriggling hand. She says she is not aware of it on her back and I should forget about it.

I never leave Eileen when we go dancing. I am so self-conscious. If I were not with Eileen I would not be going dancing. I am terrified of having to dance with anyone else. The first time we came here I literally hid behind Eileen and pretended in my mind that no one could see me. I have a good imagination and I just believed that no one could see me because Eileen is so big. I think that Eileen attracts more attention to herself than I do and people do not know I am there because they are looking at her. Always when we go dancing I head for a dark corner and wait until the floor is crowded before I ask Eileen to dance. I don't enjoy coming to this dance hall. I tremble if anyone looks at me, let alone speaks to me. Eileen always speaks to anyone who is friendly towards us; I keep my mouth shut and dance with Eileen. I am far too shy to ask any other girl to dance, although I would like to be able to do so. Unless I overcome this nervousness I am not going to make much progress. I can't rely on Eileen all my life.

Walter is the head of the dancing school and he often teaches me new steps and tries to improve my dancing. It took a long time before I would allow him to teach me because I am so terrified of embarrassing myself. When he teaches a boy to dance he holds us by the elbows and we hold him the same way.

'Walter, do you mind if I ask you something?' I say as he is teaching me some new step.

'It depends on what you want to ask.'

'Well, I think I'm doing quite well with my dancing but I feel embarrassed about my waltz hold because my hand wriggles on my partner's back and I can't control it.'

'Show me what you mean and I will try to help.'

I take hold of Walter in a waltz hold and wait for his comments.

'I can just about feel it, but had I not known about it I would not have noticed.'

Walter seems to me to be a sincere man so I believe him and feel relieved. Over and over again in varous aspects of life people assure me that my handicaps are not as noticeable as I imagine, but it always takes ages before I can accept this for myself.

We were going dancing tonight but we have met Raymond and Arthur in town and they have invited us to have a drink with them. I am afraid to go into the pub but I cannot spoil the party and I feel I must go along with them. I order a small amount of beer in a large glass which makes my three companions laugh, but they know why I did that. If I can have a large glass with only a little beer in it I will not spill my drink and I can manage quite well. I do notice that my fourth glass is easier to handle than my first. We all go dancing and I find it relatively easy to ask other girls to dance. We all partner Eileen. I have never had such a good time in my life and I wonder what has given me so much confidence.

'From now on,' says Eileen, 'we are having a drink each time before we go dancing. But I am warning you, you are not to leave me on my own. If I had not seen you tonight I would never have believed it. Alan Counsell asking strange girls to dance. I'll tell you something else you don't know – a drink improves your speech.' I am stuck for words. I feel tired and wonder if mother will be waiting up for me. If she smells beer on my breath I am sure she will not approve.

I am receiving a lot of teasing this morning from Raymond and Arthur and Joe the bundler about my escapades in the ballroom. I quite enjoy the ribbing; it sounds like being normal and for me this feels an achievement.

There is a weaver at the mill called Sabrina and Raymond is encouraging me to ask her for a date, but I am not ready yet to take girls out. However I have plucked up courage and to keep Raymond quiet I have said I will ask her out for an evening.

It is very noisy in the weaving shed and I have difficulty making conversation there so I am waiting to see Sabrina when she is away from the shed and the noise of the looms. Here she is.

'Sabrina,' I call.

She stops and waits until I get close to her and says, 'What did you call me?'

'Sabrina.'

I receive a hefty smack to my face which startles me, and I see Sabrina marching off angrily. I do not understand what promoted this attack. Raymond and Arthur laugh when I tell them about this and eventually I am told the joke. Sabrina is nicknamed behind her back, or front, after the famous 1950s' pin-up girl because they both have big busts. The weaver's real name is Jean, so no wonder she smacked my face! How do I apologize for my behaviour? Will she be prepared to listen to me? Will she understand me if I try to explain? I feel miserable, assuming that Jean has related the incident to all the girls who work with her in the mill and I dread to think what she must think of me.

It has taken several days to meet Jean away from the noise of the looms. I approach her in the comparative quiet of the room where she is replenishing her stock of weft.

'Jean, I'm sorry that I called you Sabrina. I thought that was really your name,' I say with trepidation.

'Well, I'm glad you found out my real one.'

There is a pause in our conversation, an embarrassed silence. Jean collects her weft from a large wooden crate, so large she almost has to climb into it to get it out. I am standing watching her and trying to pluck up courage to ask her out. I am feeling rather shy and nervous as Jean looks up from her task.

'Alan, why are you standing there? Don't you have any work to do?'

This puts me off and I feel more embarrassed than ever. As Jean's head disappears into the box again I shout as loud as I can to combat the sound of the mill's engine, which drifts into the weft room because the weavers constantly open the door as they come and go to collect weft.

'Jean, would you come out with me one night?' She looks at me and I feel myself going red.

'That depends on where you intend taking me.'

I feel relieved by the friendly tone of her voice. 'How about dancing on Saturday night?'

'Yes, I would like that.'

I can't believe my ears. I can't wait to tell Raymond and Arthur and hurry off to the warehouse. I realize, when I have told my friends, that I have left Jean standing in the weft room without discussing where and at what time we should meet. I really am a novice, totally unskilled where the opposite sex is concerned, but at least I am beginning to learn.

Saturday evening has come around all too soon. A confusion of feelings has kept me quiet all day. I am going out with a girl tonight and I have spent the day up until now totally terrorized by the thought of being alone with Jean. I leave early for my date remembering the effect of the beer last week. I have not the nerve to go into a pub on my own for fear of spilling or accidentally flinging my drink but I decide to go into an off-licence to buy some bottles.

All my plans are working out well. No one sees me as I leave the off-licence and go down a back street to drink. I feel confident about tonight. I feel flattered that Jean has taken so much trouble with her appearance for our meeting. She is wearing a pale blue dress with a very full skirt which makes her waist look smaller. She is also wearing make-up, and this is a surprise since she doesn't at the mill. I feel proud walking into the ballroom with her and I am glad that I put on my best navy-blue suit tonight.

I feel the evening has been a success even though I had to walk miles to get back after seeing Jean to her home.

Monday morning is a time for questioning by Raymond and Arthur, who seem to want to know all the details about Saturday evening, and especially about any kissing which took place. I am being very secretive because I did not kiss Jean. That would have required more effort and confidence than I could muster, even with the help of the beer.

I have dated Jean many times over the last few weeks and have learned a great deal about myself. She has taught me to

70

value myself a little more than I did and has proved to me that I am not too different from other boys. Always, however, I need a drink before I go out with Jean and I doubt if she is aware of this.

Having passed my elementary examination towards my City and Guilds in Textiles gives me the necessary confidence to ask if I might become a cut-looker at the mill. This request is greeted with hesitation and doubt about my abilities, but my relationship with many of the cut-lookers is such that they are willing to speak on my behalf and offer to train me. Eventually I am given a trial period as a trainee. I am sure that I can soon show that I could handle the physical side of the work but I am doubtful of my ability to handle the personnel part of the job. No one has mentioned this side of the work and I know the test will come when I am assigned looms of my own and have to deal with the employees who work in the weaving shed. But I don't need to worry about that yet, as I will be a trainee for a year. I have an ambition: to gain the final City and Guilds, but this will take three more years.

The first year has passed all too quickly and I am not prepared yet to cope with the responsibility of being assigned weavers to supervise. Even so, I am given twelve weavers and forty-eight looms, which is half of a full assignment, until I gain more experience.

I don't know why so many of the weavers are saying how happy they are to be on my list. I suspect that they might think I will be easy with them because of the relationship we had when I was a warehouse boy, or maybe it is because my handicap makes me appear less formidable than the other cut-lookers. I have a responsibility to uphold the high standards of the mill and I cannot risk losing professional respect just to be popular with weavers. I intend to be fair and just, but my weavers will soon learn that any defects in their work will be as critically treated by me as by the other cut-lookers.

It is my job to tell the weavers of any fault I find in the material they have woven and the weaver should then stop her loom until the fault is rectified. The weavers are paid waiting time while their looms are stopped, which is only half as much as weaving time, and so it is awkward when some weavers claim that they can never tell what I say as an excuse for recurring faults. I think they know exactly what I am saying, because I always show them the defective material as well. The first time a fault appears the weaver is told about it; if it appears again in the next piece of material from the same loom the weaver is fined because it would seem she has not bothered to have the cause of the defect corrected and may have wasted yards of material. It is surprising how well the weavers understand my speech and how recurring faults cease when I start to use the fining system.

The management are pleased with my efforts and I have been given a full assignment of looms. My weavers know exactly where they stand with me and think twice before trying to take advantage. However, I don't think anyone is aware of the strain and effort I face in my daily work nor how that strain seems only to respond to alcohol.

My brother Joe, who returned from the army recently, is bringing his girl home for tea today. She is very young – nearly eighteen years of age, like me.

I am interested to meet her but I can see that she is unsure of how she should react to me. I am proper and polite when she enters the house but I get no response to my greetings. She looks at me in a frightened, tense way and I wonder what she is thinking. Obviously Joe has not told her very much about me.

As I walk down the lobby to enter the parlour where Joe and his girlfriend are, I stop in my tracks as I hear their conversation.

'You need not be frightened of him. There is nothing wrong with him mentally. He doesn't speak properly, that's really all.'

'I think you should have warned me. I had no idea you had a brother like that. What's wrong with him? I hope our babies will not be the same.'

'You're being silly. I never thought to tell you about Alan. He is my brother and I don't go round making excuses for him. He has more brains than you and I put together.'

'That might be so, but you could have warned me. I felt so embarrassed when he spoke to me.'

They say that eavesdroppers never hear good of themselves and I have returned to the living room for my outdoor coat. I am going to visit Eileen so that Joe's girlfriend will not be embarrassed by my presense.

This girl has got used to me over the past few weeks and has agreed to marry Joe. I feel glad that I have not been responsible for any upset in their relationship.

The wedding has gone off very well and this time I am proud to have been a groomsman for them.

We are awaiting Joe's return from his honeymoon so that the family can see his wedding photographs. I can't remember having my photograph taken before.

The family think that the photographs are good but I am alarmed at my appearance in them. Do I really look like that? I seem to have a big stomach ... I never knew that I looked so out of shape. Mother says my appearance is caused through my bad posture and is surprised that I did not know about it. I have a very hollow back and I seem to lean backwards from the waist upwards, which throws my stomach out and makes me look fat. I feel depressed about my appearance in the wedding photographs and I wish someone could tell me what is really wrong with me. I intend to ask the doctor on my next visit.

Dr Mack is not for telling me anything about myself and I feel more and more alarmed that the only relief I get from this depression is from a drink.

I drink each lunchtime now. Not because I really like it but because I need the relaxation that it brings. It helps me to get through the afternoon. I can examine and dress cloth with the best of them but when I have to call weavers to me and do verbal battle with them and sometimes be physically threatened by them, then I need the effects of alcohol. I am becoming hardened to the comments which are made about my speech and as it is the same group of weavers who complain each day I am not too worried.

My life is quite satisfactory. I have my job, I have my

family and I have places to go in the evening. Eileen is still a very close friend but she is becoming a little tiresome in her efforts to persuade me to give up drinking. I know I rely on drink more than I should, but as I don't think I am ever actually drunk I don't see what harm I am doing. I no longer attend night school and I will not be able to get the final City and Guilds.

National Service is being discontinued but unfortunately I come into the last batch of eighteen-year-olds who will have to go before the selection panel to be called into the services. I think it is silly that someone with a body like mine should have to go for a medical. Anyone can see that I am not the right material for the forces but I have been called so I will have to go.

There is no room for any modesty or pride here. The room is full of almost naked bodies and the doctors don't care what they examine in public. I have to have an X-ray before I am seen by a panel of doctors and this is embarrassing. Five times they X-ray my chest and each time I am called back in an undignified way. A man calls out to me, 'Counsell, you moved! Come back. We need to see you again.'

I have tried to explain that I have a lot of spontaneous movement in my body which I cannot control but this man, who seems insensitive and tactless, seems to think I am shaking on purpose to keep myself out of the forces.

I have been weighed, measured, had an eye test and have been through the same examination as the rest of the boys here. Now I have to go to the tables which are placed around the room and talk to the doctors sitting there. The third doctor is looking at my back and calling other doctors over to him. My presence is ignored as if I were a mere object – I am just a back to the medical board – and the doctor is speaking to the others, regardless.

'Look at that,' he is saying. 'Do you know what you're looking at, have you seen anything like it before?'

All the doctors now look at my back. I am asked to walk, bend, stretch and move my body in every possible way while the doctors watch my back. I am in sight of everyone in the room and quite naked.

74

'You can get dressed now, son, you won't be needed again,' says the first doctor.

'Does that mean I won't be called up?' I ask.

'No, no. You're no good to your country. You won't be called up,' answers the doctor with a laugh. I feel humiliated.

Dr Mack is still not too disturbed about my drinking but then I have not told him how much I regularly put away. Anyway, just the other day Dr Mack finally told me what was really wrong with me and if the shock of the knowledge that I am a brain-damaged spastic doesn't warrant a drink, I don't know what does.

In my bedroom drawer I keep a bottle of whisky and have reached the point where I need a shot of it before breakfast each morning otherwise I feel limp and quite useless. After my first drink I am able to go through until midday and then after a lunchtime drink or two it is quite easy to go through until the evening and the pubs open again.

I can't quite remember when I began taking drink to work. Each breaktime I have whisky from my flask, but I don't think anyone knows and I can still do my work. I never have any complaints.

How Dr Mack has finally found out how much I drink I will never know. Maybe there are physical signs to recognize, or perhaps Eileen has told him, but now, all of a sudden, he has the same old speech to make week after week. 'Cut down on your drinking. You are going to ruin your health.' I am not really interested in what he says and I have decided not to go and see him again anyway.

Life is quite pleasant as I drink my way through problems and fears. Any comments about my speech or handicap do not penetrate anymore. I can face anything as long as I have a bottle with me. No one but Eileen ever mentions my drinking habits and so I imagine that no one else knows how much I drink. But Eileen says everyone knows because I am constantly drunk. I don't believe her and I don't care anyway.

Eileen has now got a job as book-keeper at the mill where I work and on the first morning she has taken away my flask. I know it is her because it has never been taken before. I have

75

to go without a drink until lunchtime. It seems ever such a long morning and by the end of it I am feeling very shaky but a drink during lunchtime is helping me to feel steady again. Eileen is going on terribly about it all and is marshalling my activities. Each morning she checks my flask and each lunchtime she comes with me to the pub and raises the roof if I have more than one drink. Mother is preparing a packed lunch for Eileen now and Eileen virtually drags me away from the pub at midday. She seems obsessed with keeping me off the bottle. Eileen is also keen for me to start going to see Dr Mack again each week but I don't see the point. She even says she will go with me, because she thinks I ought to speak to him about my alcoholism. I think this is the height of absurdity; surely if I were as bad as Eileen says, mother would be on my back as well. I start to regard Eileen as a real troublemaker; she is threatening to tell my mother how much I drink if I don't cut down.

Finally, I can see that Eileen nags out of solicitude. She has got through to me and I am limiting my drinking to the evenings, but I do find my work hard without it.

Eileen thinks it may help if I have something to look forward to and has talked me into booking a holiday in the Isle of Man. As I have no really close friends apart from her I am going on my own, and I am viewing this holiday as a challenge. While I have been drinking I have isolated myself from others, preferring alcohol to friends; even Raymond and Arthur have become estranged from me. Eileen has been my companion for the last few weeks helping me to cut down and I have taken a little less alcohol each day. I can manage with as little as four pints of beer and a whisky per night! But I find I am a lot more sensitive to people's reactions towards my handicap and very often feel like turning back to the bottle for shelter.

Mother is alarmed when she knows that I have been drinking heavily for months. Each morning she has been in the bakehouse when I have got up and when I tottered home late in the evening she would be in bed, so she hardly saw me. Now that I am not drinking so much Eileen has told mother the whole story so that between them they can keep me dry.

It has not been easy and were it not for the fact that I finally agreed with Eileen and confessed that I did have a drink problem, I would never have managed to cut down. My hands shake much more now, but I am hoping that this will stop as my body adjusts to being without alcohol. I feel jittery inside as well, but that too is because I am fighting my drinking.

Now that my thought processes are clearer as the alcohol leaves my system, I begin to think about my appearance on my brother's wedding photographs and seek ways to improve my posture. I write to 'Max Alding' the famous body-builder and ask if he can help. He plans a training routine for me and I have to exercise morning and evening. The exercises are difficult at first but become easier with practice. I have to begin with a moderate effort and as I get more used to using my muscles I have to make them really work and contract them forcibly.

Exercises each day are boring but I can feel an improvement. I am sure that I walk more erectly. I suffer a crisis of confidence. I have always thought that my speech was the only outward sign of my handicap and I have not been aware of my posture defect. I feel so self-conscious as I walk about, thinking that I look handicapped.

Lots of people at the mill are saying how much better I look and how glad they are to see me without a drink inside me, so I find my confidence returning. Even now I am naïve enough to think that as my posture improves so my handicap is hidden; once again I fool myself into thinking that I appear normal.

I don't have many friends, although I go to the cinema now and again with Raymond and Arthur. But we seem to have grown apart, which is my fault, as while I was drinking I had no time for people.

Eileen is keen to take up ballroom dancing seriously and try for medals, so I am going along with her. Dancing seems to be one thing I do reasonably well. Both Eileen and I have been accepted into the crowd at the dancing school quite easily once I have overcome my initial shyness and self-consciousness. When I went dancing in recent months I always had a bellyful of booze and didn't feel shy, but now I have to relearn social integration without the prop of drink. It isn't easy at first and many times I want to escape from the academy. But I know I have to overcome my feelings of inferiority and awkwardness and force myself to go each week. I used only to dance with Eileen, but they are a friendly crowd there and although it has taken a time for me to respond to their warmth, I have friends and other partners too, now.

I used to feel uneasy when I had to dance with a stranger during a teaching session; the dancing instructor likes us to dance with different partners, as he thinks it bad if we are only able to dance with one person. Dancing has helped me to form relationships, firstly without speaking, and it has not taken me long to find my tongue while I am dancing. Both Eileen and I have various partners for different dances. A girl called Pearl is my partner for Latin American dances and it is marvellous to be able to dance well enough to make other people watch us. My confidence is growing through dancing and so I find the need to drink decreased.

It is time for my holiday in the Isle of Man. I have booked into a hotel in Ramsey that has a ballroom. All my meals are going to be served in my room so that I will not suffer the embarrassment of having to eat in public.

This is my first experience of a posh holiday hotel; I have arrived early in the morning after an overnight journey. The boat was crowded coming over and I felt a bit lonesome as I travelled alone. Most of the other passengers were holiday-makers and were obviously in good spirits, but I was full of concern about whether the venture was a good idea for me to make on my own.

I have been shown to my hotel room and expect to wait about two hours before breakfast is served. I should really sleep, but I feel too excited now that I have rid myself of many negative thoughts about not making friends. As I have unpacked my things I am going for a walk along the beach.

I have an Irish maid who will be serving all my meals and she is very friendly and chatty. She is concerned because I am all on my own but I explain that I am quite all right and hope to make some friends before the end of the week.

The hotel ballroom is frequented by older people and I feel conspicuous sitting here on my own. One man has been over to speak to me. He is, coincidentally, from my home town and he used to go around with my Aunty May when he was younger. He tells me that Aunty May used to carry a large hatpin around with her and used it forcibly if boys got too close. No wonder Aunty May never married!

My Irish maid is on duty in the ballroom tonight taking orders for drinks, and she speaks to me as I leave the ballroom. 'Is it an early night for you then?' she asks.

'There is no one of my age to dance with, so I think I will go and read a book for a while,' I reply.

Later there is a knock on my bedroom door, and I put down my book.

'Who is there?' I ask through the door.

'It's me,' comes the reply. I open the door and there stands my Irish maid with a young man. 'This is George, one of the hotel cooks. We are off duty and are on our way to the staff club. We thought you might like to join us.'

'That is very kind of you, but I was thinking about turning in for the night.'

'There will be lots of young people there. You will be very welcome.'

'Well, what are we waiting for? Thank you for asking me. My name is Alan, by the way.'

'Good, I'm glad you will come with us. My name is Patsy.'

I follow them through the hotel and down into the cellar where there are a few more young people dancing and talking. Patsy introduces me and I soon find myself amidst a compatible company and plenty of dancing partners.

At around one in the morning I am invited to go for a dip in the sea, but as I cannot swim I just go along to watch the fun.

I am invited to join these young people on their days off and I enjoy my holiday enormously. I feel rather chuffed as I return home on the boat for although Patsy made the first move, I have made friends in the Isle of Man and my holiday was a success. If I can travel all that way and make friends in a

79

strange place surely I could meet more people in my home town?

I have a test ahead. My parents are planning a big party for my twenty-first birthday and have invited all my relatives and friends. I do not know quite how I feel about this as I have not seen many of my relations for years and some of them I do not even know. Personally I would have preferred a small affair but I cannot disappoint mother and father.

The night of my party is wet and I am concerned about getting my new black suit drenched as I wait for the taxi. I have to be at the hall early to greet all our guests. This is daunting. The comments I am hearing from some of my relatives, particularly those whom I have not seen for years, are embarrassing. I do not know what some of these people thought I might grow up into, but if my own family can feel this way about me then the general public may have some excuse. An uncle, for example, greets me with a silly, surprised voice.

'Well, Alan, don't we look smart? I would never have known it was you, you do look well.'

He goes on his way talking to his wife without giving me the chance to reply. As they retreat I hear him say, 'He cannot speak to me. I never know what he is saying, but I must say he has grown up better than I thought he would.'

I feel crestfallen and cannot believe such rudeness. How can he speak like that about me? The last time I saw him I was only ten years old, so how can he know that he can never tell what I say? I'm still too young to realize that in this exchange lies the whole, crucial dilemma of my life: that I must learn to tolerate and understand other people's responses to me as well as accepting myself. Progress will be hard until that lesson is truly learned.

We ought to feel honoured tonight because an aunt and uncle are coming to the party who have always thought themselves to be a bit too good for the likes of us and have separated themselves from the family. Here they come now, and this time I am ready.

'Good evening, Aunty Doris, I have never met you, but I know who you are.'

80

She looks at me as though I had no right to speak to her and says to her husband, 'Who is this person?'

He replies, 'This is Alan.'

Aunty is looking round the room and answers, 'I thought he could not talk. Look, there is your sister, let's join her.'

They walk away and leave me feeling snubbed; neither of them actually spoke to me. Some of my relatives are ashamed of me, but I mustn't feel sorry for myself.

Here come mother and father. 'Alan, we must start the dancing. Who do you think could start it off for us?'

Traditionally in our family, the person whose party it is always starts off the dancing, but obviously mother and father do not think I am capable. I think this is going to be the night for a few surprises. 'Mother, the dancing can wait five minutes and I will begin it. Olive will be my partner, but first I must find Eileen and have a drink. Could you find Olive for me?'

Mother is straightening my tie and saying, 'Are you sure you can dance in front of all these people?'

I do not even answer but give her a peck on the cheek and wink at my father. As I hurry off I ask her again to find Olive.

I find Eileen with the crowd I have invited from the dancing academy. 'Right, Eileen, I need your help. I am certain that half of the people here think I am a half-wit, and I intend to change their minds. Would you go and get me a stiff drink? I'm going to open the dancing by dancing with Olive. Even mother and father don't think I can do that.'

'Oh, Alan, do you need a drink? Go on, we will be behind you.'

I am not in the mood for arguments. 'Eileen, I need a drink and I don't want to ask anyone else to get me one. Now, please help. I promise I will only have the one. Go to the bar for me quickly, a double whisky.'

Eileen goes to the bar and returns with my drink. I am in such a state that she has to hold the glass to my lips for me. But I do feel better afterwards. Olive is waiting with father by the band and I join them.

'Right, Olive, can you do a waltz?'

'Yes, of course I can.'

'Then what are we waiting for?'

The band strikes up and I lead Olive round the floor deliberately like a raw beginner. Halfway round and Olive is amazed as I say, 'Now, let's really waltz.'

I lengthen my stride and lead Olive into whisks and wings and open tallies and chassés. I am really enjoying this – the floor to myself and a captive audience.

The dance is ended and Olive says, 'Alan, I didn't know you could dance like that. You are a dark horse.'

'You have not seen anything yet.'

I leave the floor and make my way to Eileen and my friends from the dancing academy to the astonishment and applause of many of the guests. Mother and father are looking amazed and are following me. As they join our group they express surprise at my dancing and are as proud as peacocks. The band is playing a barn dance. I must ask my Aunty Elsie to partner me for this because it is the first dance I ever learned and she taught it to me.

Aunty Elsie is delighted, and obviously aware of the attitude of some of the people in the room. 'You made a few people stare as you danced with Olive.'

'Yes, aunty, I know, and I intend to make a few more stare before tonight is through.'

'I know how you feel, but don't get a chip on your shoulder. Many of these people do not really know you and have not seen you very often. I am sure they are really delighted to see you are doing so well. Many of us did not know how you were going to be when you grew up and we are so proud of you. Don't spoil it by being aggressive. Just be yourself and allow those who have a wrong impression to change it.'

I can see aunty is right and that maybe I have no reason to be angry.

The band is playing a Latin American selection and I am being paged by the group from the dancing academy to dance with Pearl. This will make a few eyes pop.

I am aware of my brother John watching me dance and he is obviously amazed. He is now coming over to speak to me and I ask him, 'Are you enjoying yourself?'

There is an odd look in his eye. 'Am I enjoying myself? Alan, to see you dance like that is more than enjoyment to me, it's a real thrill.'

'Well, John, I have been dancing for a considerable time now. Did you expect me just to stumble round the floor?'

'I have never thought about *how* you danced. I've not seen you dance. The family have often wondered what you got up to when you went to that dance class but we never thought that you, of all people, could be so good.'

While we are standing at the bar later, I introduce John and his wife to my friends and have several more drinks. I do not normally drink like this nowadays but tonight is a special occasion and I know I have to make a speech before long. This frightens me a little, although Eileen and I have practised what I am going to say. I know a drink can take away the fluttering feeling from my stomach and that I will be all right. I can see people congregating round the buffet, which means father is ready to make his speech. No one is expecting much from me but I intend to follow the family tradition.

As I leave the company in the bar to go and find Eileen I am grabbed by the arm and confronted by Dr Mack, who I did not know had been asked to the party.

'Are you not going to speak to me now that you are a man in your own right?'

'Dr Mack, how nice to see you! I'm so glad you were able to come. How long have you been here?'

'We have only just arrived. You are looking very smart. Are you going to have a drink with me?'

'Later, if you don't mind. I think mother and father are wanting me over there right now.'

As I proceed across the room I am met by Eileen, who seems to be suffering from worse nerves than me. 'Alan, it is time for your speech, are you all right? Will you be able to do it?'

'Yes, I'm all right. You go and have a drink – it will calm your nerves – but be quick. I need you there in case I dry up!'

We have reached mother and father and Eileen is offered a sherry.

'Come on, father, let's get this over. You have a speech to make and then I will make one.'

'That won't be necessary; no one expects you to make a speech.' My father is saying what he thought best.

'It's no use worrying or arguing. I am all rehearsed and ready to go.'

Father is looking at mother with a look which says, What next? and proceeds to gain the attention of the guests. After the toast and after the singing of 'For he's a jolly good fellow' I get to my feet. I hear Eileen saying, 'Don't forget, make the sound come through the top of your head.' Advice from Miss Nuttall! I deliver the rehearsed speech and feel panic throughout. What if they can't tell a word of what I am saying?

My speech is over, mother has been presented with her bouquet and father with cigars. I am embraced by Olive and mother and several others who all have tears in their eyes. Then my mother speaks to me. 'I never thought I would live to see the day when you made a speech like that.'

I don't think I said anything special enough to warrant this tearful affection, but Eileen is saying that people were moved at the clearness of my words rather than by what I said. The dancing continues and I have a good time showing off my fanciest steps and mixing with as many guests as possible.

It is now almost one o'clock the following afternoon and mother has brought me tea in bed. I suppose it was very late when we returned from the party, but I am surprised that I have slept so long.

'Good morning, mother. Look at the time! Why didn't you waken me?'

'No need. You need your rest after last night.'

'Yes, it was quite a party.'

'Yes, Alan, quite a party. I must say your father and I were pleasantly shocked.'

'Shocked, mother? In what way shocked?'

'Alan, I think you are a very dark horse. We had a job to get you to walk and then we see you dancing the way you did last night. We couldn't believe our eyes. Why didn't you

84

tell us how well you could dance?'

'Mother, I am not that good. I never thought to discuss my dancing with you.'

'We knew you went dancing but we thought that you just did your best. We never imagined you could do all those fancy bits.'

'I'm not that special, mother. I could be better.'

'Alan, you don't understand. We have raised you thinking that you were going to be less able than the average person. It just shows that father and I don't really know you. That speech you gave – it was so clear. I don't think anyone in that room was in any doubt as to what you said. I don't know how you did it, but it was good.'

Mother has left me and I consider the things she said. I am astonished to reconsider my progress, to remember that I have come from being dragged to school because I could not walk to being able to dance confidently in public. I begin to think about the speech I made at the party yesterday. It is marvellous that I have been able to address a gathering and, most of all, be understood. Reflecting on these things makes me feel quite emotional. Suddenly life seems exciting and full of potential.

There are lots of changes at the mill with the introduction of synthetic materials and I am learning new techniques in dressing these fabrics. There are not yet many looms weaving synthetic fabrics but their numbers are increasing all the time.

My confidence has grown to the extent that I now take driving lessons. My instructor, Brenda, is the daughter of one of my primary-school teachers. Gary, her husband, takes me for a lesson now and again and we get along together really well. It's funny how sometimes one takes to a stranger instantly, as though one has been friends for years. I'm afraid I didn't pass my test, but in addition to the driving lessons Gary and I sometimes go shooting together on Sunday mornings. The first time I shot the gun I'd no idea where the slug went. Now with many weeks of practice my aim is somewhat better, although I never ever bag anything. It's enjoyable just to roam the woods with a friend. Gary will never go to a pub and I suspect there is a strong reason for this. Whenever drink is mentioned I can sense tension.

It has taken Gary six months to confide in me. Today he told me that he had just returned from hospital when we first met, where he had been treated for alcoholism. I think Gary was very surprised to hear of my drinking problem of a few years ago, not that I was as bad as he had been. I can see how fortunate I was to be saved from an addiction that was only adding to my handicap.

On reflection, my relationship with Gary has been special, as he actually needed my companionship and sought my company. When he returned from hospital he had lost a lot of confidence and, I suspect, some of his self-esteem. Curiously enough he has said that through my acceptance of him he has found his confidence and thinks better of himself. I am amazed that I could be of help in this way to anyone.

Seventy per cent of the looms at the mill are now weaving synthetic fibres. For some reason I keep having time away from work with bronchitis. This chestiness has continued for many weeks and I don't seem to be getting any better. Finally, when I have been away from work for three months and each time I visit the mill to see my workmates my breathing becomes worse, I learn the truth. I am suffering from asthma caused by an allergy to synthetic yarns, so I have to leave the mill. This represents a real blow, as the mill has been the place of most of my major transitions from childhood to adulthood.

Indeed the mill has been a place of great learning and education. I have learned to cope independently and to respond positively to the difficult aspects of other people's reactions to me.

The personal progress I feel I have made whilst working there has been tremendous and I shall forever be indebted to the people who worked with me and who cared enough to correct many of my bad habits. They taught me much merely by accepting me and allowing me to become part of their

86

world. I am over my drinking problem and now that I have continued to hold down a responsible job supervising my weavers, I realize what a tremendous difference this has made to my self-image. I am going to miss my work at the mill but I am sure that it has prepared me for future life.

Being unemployed is tedious and demoralizing. There is no work for me and I am to be given a medical next week by some ministry doctor to see whether my disablement claim is legitimate.

The ministry doctor's report has been sent to Dr Mack and I have to come and see what it says. The doctor tells me that it is not usual for the patient to see the report, but he will read bits of it out to me. He wants to see my reaction because the report says I am unable to use public transport, unable to feed myself unaided and unable to live away from home. I feel angry because the ministry doctor only saw me for about ten minutes and these judgements are going to affect my entire future. The report has been sent to the disablement resettlement officer who is supposed to help me in finding a new job.

'Here I am and here I will stay until that medical report is removed from my records and destroyed.'

I have been sitting in the office of the disablement resettlement officer for about two hours and each time I am asked to leave I repeat this litany. Of course, I don't expect they can help, but at least I am making my point. How dare that doctor write such a report when he hardly looked at me? He asked my age, name and address and nothing more. I intend seeing Barbara Castle, who is the Member of Parliament for Blackburn, but this does not impress the people at the labour exchange.

I have been sitting here all day and now at three in the afternoon they have brought the area officer to speak to me. He is saying that I should not know what my medical report says.

'But I do, and there are "facts" down on that report which are wrong and I object to them and I want the report destroyed.' I am furious.

'We can't just destroy a report because you don't agree with it,' says the man in charge.

'Look, that report is incorrect. I can feed myself without any help. I use public transport every day and I feel confident that I could live on my own if I had to,' I reply.

'All right, you have made your point and I will mark your record accordingly.'

'That is not good enough for me. I want every copy of that report destroyed. What if a job came up for me but to get to it I had to use public transport? Would you send me for it? No, because my medical records tells you I am unable to use public transport.'

The man looks at me wearily. 'But I can't destroy the report.'

'Well, what can you do? In my opinion my records contain incorrect information and I would like it put right. I intend to sit here until you do something.'

'But we are closing the office now.'

'Then I'll be back in the morning.'

I have spent three days sitting in this office and have had the same conversation each day. But tomorrow I have an appointment to see Barbara Castle and I am hoping she will have a solution.

The familiar red hair and the green suit with the white flowing bow at the neck are exactly what I imagined I would see when I met her. She is charming and her smile puts me at ease. She is interested to know the background of my complaint and asks if I have had other medicals with the Ministry of Labour.

I tell her about the first medical I had (to register as a disabled person), how I was told then that I was unfit and unable to work and how my mother had got my first job for me. I describe the progress I had made in the mill.

Mrs Castle listens sympathetically and seems concerned. She is going to write a letter on my behalf to the divisional disablement resettlement officer and if I don't hear anything within the next two weeks I am to contact her secretary again.

It is only five days since my interview with Barbara Castle and the disablement resettlement officer has sent for me to say that my medical records are to be destroyed and that I have to have another medical.

5

The people at the labour exchange depress and frustrate me because they keep referring to a very early medical report, from the doctor who saw me when I was fifteen, at the time when I had first to register as a disabled person. It states that I am unfit for employment because of my physical disabilities. The clerks and officers at the labour exchange ignore the fuss made over my last medical. I had thought that all my medical records had been destroyed because of Barbara Castle's intervention but this doesn't seem to be the case. They are still saying that I am unemployable. I have worked in the mill for almost seven years; is this not proof that I am capable of earning my own living?

There are interesting-sounding jobs advertised in our local paper but when I inquire about them I am always told that because I am unemployed I need a card from the labour exchange. When I ask for one I am told that they cannot introduce me to a possible employer because my records say that I am unfit for work. And so it goes on.

After many weeks of argument the disablement resettlement officer has agreed to send me for an assessment to a government rehabilitation unit so that, if all goes well, the label 'unemployable' can be erased at last from my records.

Eventually, after another wait of about three weeks, I have arrived at a unit in Leicester where I stay in a dormitory with eleven other men. I do not enjoy this, or the company of some of my fellow residents. The man who sleeps in the next bed to me has lost both his legs and one arm and he is obviously mentally disturbed as well. While I feel sorry for him I would not choose to live with him, for the most prosaic

90

of reasons. He wakes everyone up in the night with his screams as he relives in his nightmares his motorbike accident. Another man has lost the function of his bowel and has to wear a bag. He is not fussy where he leaves his used bags and the smell is awful. There is a younger person in the corner bed who is homosexual. While he has the right to do what he wants with his life I do not see why I should have to tolerate his advances.

After four weeks of tests in the joinery department, the light engineering section, and the painting and decorating department and after being subjected to many assessments by the unit's psychologist, it has been decided that I should train as a gardener's labourer. I don't enjoy gardening. I dream uneasily of insects and worms and although I am not actually frightened by them I need only close my eyes after a day of digging the garden to be haunted by the creatures who live in the soil.

I have tried to explain this but I am told by my supervisor that I will get used to it. I have asked if I can go home as I do not feel that this course is useful, but I am advised not to do so as that would put a black mark on my record at the Ministry of Labour.

After twelve weeks my course is over and I return home. My family welcomes me as if I had been gone for years.

I have to attend the labour exchange this morning and I am sitting waiting with hope and anticipation at the thought that now I might be offered a job. I expect to be found a gardening job, and although I dislike this work I dislike the fact of not having a job even more. The disablement resettlement officer is telling me that gardening posts in this area are very few and far between and that my chances of getting this type of work are slim. And so I wait.

As I look in the evening paper today I see an advertisement:

National charity require person to act as escort to foreign visitors investigating the English system of caring for the handicapped. Training will be given for this temporary appointment.

I apply to a London post-office box number even though my

mother and father don't like the idea – I am fed up with sitting around with nothing to do but help in the bakehouse now and again.

I have received a letter in the post this morning calling me to an interview and giving me more details of the job. If I am lucky enough to be appointed I shall be living in a hotel in London during the weeks I am required to work. I will have to meet foreign visitors as they enter the country, take them around England to visit various establishments which care for the handicapped, and explain the function of each place. Apparently all the visitors will speak English or have an interpreter with them. Initially I would be required to spend three weeks in London to study each centre on the itinerary to learn its history and work. I would be employed by the International Society for the Welfare of Crippled Children.

Although it is an exciting prospect I don't feel that I have the confidence necessary for such a job. Still, I will have to pluck up courage and travel to London, as I don't have any other options. I explained all about myself when I applied for the job so the people who have sent for me have some idea of the kind of person I am. Surely if I can cope with going to the Isle of Man and Leicester on my own I can travel to London for an interview?

If I think of how I might manage to do such a job I feel real panic so I must not allow my thoughts to go beyond the interview itself.

Others might make a little less of going for a meeting in London, but I have all kinds of fears. Not having been there before I wonder how I will react to a busy city. What to do about food is another worry. As I will be travelling overnight I do not like the idea of taking sandwiches. Since I may be away from home for twenty-four hours, I feel such snacks may not be adequate. The long train journey will add complications too: I find it difficult to eat and drink when I am motionless, so the jogging of the train could be disastrous.

I have decided to buy a new suit for the interview as I am sure my confidence will increase if I am looking the best I can. The cashier in the bank where I went this morning to get money for my suit must think I'm an idiot. I tried to sign the withdrawal form with a fountain pen, which was silly because I can write more easily with a biro. The ink would not flow so I shook it to try and get the ink to the nib; then it came out, all of it, a big blob on the floor of the bank.

'I am sorry, I have made a puddle on the floor. Do you have a mop please?' I asked the cashier.

'What do you mean, you have made a puddle on the floor?' asked the cashier, her face registering absolute disgust.

'No, not that. All the ink has come out of my pen on to your floor and I would like something to clean it up with,' I explain. The relief on the cashier's face confirmed that she had thought that I had wetted the floor myself. I may be over-sensitive but once again I wonder if it was just my impeded speech (as well as my obvious physical handicap) that led her to think that way. Or could it be that I am, in a more complicated way, language-handicapped, that I used the wrong word structure in my request? So much which comes naturally to most still seems terribly and dauntingly sophisticated to me. When I am speaking to people, I often find that I should have worded things differently, to make what I am saying clearer.

It is almost time for me to leave home to get the 9.30 overnight train to London. I do not know who is in a worse state, me or mother. If she knew how scared I really feel she would not allow me to go, but I am putting every effort into appearing calm and relaxed. Mother has a thousand don'ts for me: don't let people see your money, don't play cards on the train with strangers, don't go to sleep on the train without first making sure people cannot get at your money. It is impossible to remember all her don'ts and I think she is a little too fussy.

I have it all worked out. I get into Euston at 6.30 a.m. and I am going to get my breakfast in a café behind the station that Eileen has told me about; then I will return to the station to change into my new suit and leave my case in the left-luggage office. After that I will have a little time to look around before my interview at ten o'clock.

I have found the café which Eileen told me about but I am not finding it easy to go inside. Being so early in the morning I thought it might be empty but I was wrong, it is full of people. I just don't have the confidence to walk in and have breakfast. I am walking around the block hoping that the café will empty. It is silly. I am hungry and I have two options: either I stay hungry or I can pluck up courage and walk into the café and order. There are tables free where I could sit on my own and there is a waitress, so I would not need to carry anything to my table. If I were to do anything embarrassing it would not matter as no one knows me around here. After telling myself all this I take a deep breath and walk in. I have found a table in the corner and the waitress is approaching to take my order. I am having to repeat myself for the fourth time as the waitress cannot understand me but I must not allow that to bother me. All that matters is that ultimately I have got a breakfast.

What a feeling of achievement. I have travelled to London, ordered and eaten a meal in a public place and changed my clothes. Usually my mother has to help me to button my shirt neck and cuffs and sometimes to tie my shoe laces, but here I am looking quite smart and feeling comfortably fed – all through my own efforts.

The next step is to find a taxi and get to my interview. I hesitated for so long before I went into the café earlier this morning and it has taken me quite a while to dress myself, so nearly all the time has gone. It doesn't matter, though. I can have a look around London after my interview.

Three other people are in the waiting room. I had problems with the receptionist on my way in as she thought I said my name was Thompson, but after I spelled it out for her she found it on her list. The waiting room is quiet and everyone looks tense. What chance have I? All of these people look far more able than I feel I am and I cannot understand why I have been called here against such odds. The longer I sit here the less confident I feel.

The first woman to be called for her interview has just returned to the waiting room looking flushed. She is gathering up her things ready to leave. She was in the

94

interview room just ten minutes and it seemed an age.

My name is being called and I am being shown into the interview room. There are two men and a woman waiting to see me. I feel ill at ease when I first enter the room, but these people are very nice and skilled in making people feel relaxed. As I answer their questions I remember that I need to make my voice come through the top of my head to give my speech more clarity. I have answered many questions and have discussed the problems which I may face while I am living away from home. I must say I think that I have spoken with a lot more confidence than I actually feel. I have been asked to take a seat in the waiting room as I may be needed again. I do not know what this means; the woman who was called in for an interview just before me was not asked to wait, so why was I?

Sitting here I have watched the third person leave and go home and now the fourth person has returned and is also waiting. It is nerve-racking sitting here. It is quiet and time seems to be passing so slowly. My stomach muscles are twitching violently. They always do when I am nervous but today I can see myself jerking around the middle of my body. We have been sitting here for about twenty minutes and I am beginning to think that we have been forgotten. The other man has been called in again and I am left alone in the room.... That did not last long – the other man has returned to the waiting room after only a few minutes and is preparing to leave the building. Now I am being called in once again.

'Come and sit down, Mr Counsell. We are sorry you have had such a long wait but these things take time, don't they?' says the woman as I enter.

I sit on the chair in front of the desk facing the three people who interviewed me earlier and try to conceal my wriggling hand by hiding it between my crossed thighs.

'Well Mr Counsell, we have decided to offer you a position and would like you to begin next Monday,' says one of the men. The three of them have risen from their chairs and are offering their hands in congratulation.

I am stunned and speechless. I cannot believe it. I know

I am being addressed but the words will not penetrate, I am so shocked.

Outside on the pavement I feel sick and I can feel my body trembling. I do not know whether this is because the interview is over or whether it is the realization of what I've let myself in for. My mind is in turmoil; I am to leave home and live in London and be trained for a job which will require me to meet strangers and take them around the country. I am going to need much more confidence than I feel at the moment. I am going to try very hard to make a success out of this extraordinary opportunity.

Wandering around London and looking at some of the places which have just been familiar names to me has eased my tension a bit, and now I am feeling hungry again. If I am going to begin work in London I had better get used to being independent; I am not going to repeat my breakfast performance. The first café I see I am going to walk into, no matter how crowded it is, and order a meal. If I can act with confidence then maybe I will appear more normal. I must have looked odd this morning as I walked around and around, continually coming back to look inside that café.

Somehow I am in Baker Street and there is a café down a side street. No uncertainty this time. I walk through the door and sit at a table. I'm pleased: I did not look to see how many people were in before entering nor did I look at the menu in the window. The waiter has come for my order and rather than say it to him I am showing him the menu and pointing to what I would like to eat. I must say it is quicker to order this way than to try and get the waiter to understand my speech.

Today has been one of the best in my life for increasing my confidence. It could be the start of something new. I do not know how I am going to cope with foreign visitors nor how I am going to manage living away from home in London, but other people have shown their faith in me and I will do my best. Doubts and inadequacies must be hidden.

Looking round London has been fun and I am hoping that while I am working here in the next few months, I can visit many more sights. All the time I keep thinking how truly amazing it is that I have done so much today without real

My mother and father in 1928

Above When I was three

Right Aunty Elsie

Left Mammy and Papa
Earnshaw in 1950

Below Mother and father in
1952

Above Mother, Alan, Tom and nephew Jim at Blackpool in 1955

Left Alan in 1954

Below With Olive, 1953

Audley Hall Mill, Blackburn

Arthur, Pearl, Dennis, Sheila (Arthur's wife) and Alan at the
dancing academy, 1956

Above Arthur

Above right Olive

Above Raymond

Right Eileen on her wedding day
in 1961. She had lost eight
stones in weight

Above Alan Counsell in 1982

Top left Alan and Kathleen with baby Grant in 1968

Middle left Alan with Grant at nine months

Left Grant, three, with Marcia, four weeks

Right At the typewriter. The keys are depressed with a pencil and each page takes nearly an hour

Below Teaching at Oliver Wells School

The Counsell family, 1982,
Kathleen, Marcia, Grant, Emma and Alan

embarrassment or hitch. I am even more amazed that I have been appointed to such an attractive and demanding job.

Of course mother and father are waiting to hear the news on my return. They are both working in the bakehouse, as it is late. My news is greeted with silence and I cannot read the looks which my parents are exchanging. I would have expected them to be delighted that I had got the job, but mother is worried about me living away from home. 'Alan, how will you manage?'

'Mother, I will be all right, I will be living in a hotel. The hotel will supply my breakfast and evening meals and I will have lunch at the office.'

'That sounds an expensive way to live to me. Who is paying for all this?'

'Mother, stop worrying. It all goes with the job. The firm pays all my expenses and I receive a wage for each week I work.'

'But, Alan, you are not used to living in hotels and you are certainly not used to meeting strangers. I don't think you should accept the job. You are biting off more than you can chew.'

'Mother, I am going to give it a try. I know I can do it. If I fail it won't be because I have not tried. And I know I can always come back home. I have had enough of being out of work. I have never been offered a job, and was frank at my interview about my difficulties. Now if the people who interviewed me are prepared to take me on, the least I can do is give it a try. They did not think my speech would cause too many problems and since the visitors will be interested in handicapped people in Britain it might be a good idea to have a handicapped person as their escort.'

Father interrupts with a little laugh, 'Mamma, you are just wasting your breath. The lad has made up his mind and you know as well as I that it is no use arguing with him. I feel proud of him and I think it is amazing that he has gone off on his own and got this job. I do wonder what the hell we have brought up. Let him go to bed and we'll talk about it in the morning.'

I leave the bakehouse with two hot crumpets in my hand

and go into the house to prepare for bed. I love crumpets straight from the hotplate with so much butter on them that it runs through the holes, and as I sit by the dying fire to eat them my mother comes into the house.

'Alan, what *are* you going to do next? You put years on me. I have been worried sick all day wondering if you were all right in London on your own and thinking you would return home all depressed and disappointed because you had not got the job. And here you are as calm as you please, telling me that you are leaving home for a while to go and work in London. I don't think your father or I would have the confidence to do that, so I don't know how you can do it!'

'I will be all right, please don't fuss.'

After I have finished my supper I go upstairs to bed, followed by mother. I can never remember her tucking me into bed before but she does so tonight.

It's like a family reunion. Every member of my family has come from their work to see how I got on in London yesterday. Everyone is amazed and excited that I got the job. I am being made to feel as though I have done the deed of the year. Anyone would think that they had got the job instead of me. I feel overwhelmed. How can I fail in anything I do with such tremendous people behind me?

Father is in bed as is usual at this time of day, as he works through the night. We usually have to creep around the house so as not to disturb him. If he is awakened by any noise from the family he is terribly angry, but today is different. He has been awakened by all the noise after only two hours' sleep and there is complete silence from each of us as he comes downstairs. We await the explosion. But he greets us in a congenial way and announces that the occasion calls for a bottle to be opened. This has never been known before, as mother does not allow drink in the house. Where the bottle has come from I do not know, but I feel like a film star as I am toasted and congratulated by my family.

The disablement resettlement officer is not pleased with me. When I told him I had got a job and would not be signing on next week he produced a form which he said had to be filled in. The form seemed to me to be giving credit to the labour exchange for finding me work and I did not like that. I am disappointed in the help I have been given there and I do not want to give the top people the idea that my new position was secured by any help from the Blackburn office of the Ministry of Labour. Of course they have an answer for everything. Unless the form is filled in my insurance card will not be sent on. I have to fill the form in but I am adding very boldly that the appointment has been made through my own efforts and not through any help from the department.

All the family want me to visit them in their homes on Sunday before I leave for London on Monday morning. This is impossible so Olive has invited everyone to tea on Sunday. All this fuss and bother. Anyone would think I was going away never to return. I am only going to London, and I may even return at the weekend.

Father is giving me his electric razor to take with me. He says it will be easier and quicker for me, as I have to take extra care shaving because I cut myself easily. He didn't bother when I went to Leicester but I suppose there is more sense of occasion this time. Father also left a package in my room this morning. It contained cufflinks. They are unusual in that they have an expanding chain in between their two golden buttons so I can put them into my cuffs before I put my shirt on. This means that the trouble I have in buttoning my cuffs will be eliminated. Mother has altered all my shirts so that there is a buttonhole each side of my cuff.

At last I am away. Now that I am on my own and the experience has begun, it is difficult to employ my new determination to pretend to be confident in all situations and at all times. I feel conspicuous with my case at my feet. It is in the way of the other passengers but it is far too heavy for me to lift up on to the luggage rack. I tried to put it in the guard's van but it was closed. As I am travelling I am thinking of all that may lie before me: somehow the worst thing is going to be eating in the hotel dining room.

Miss Partridge, one of the people who interviewed me, is at the station to meet me. She takes me to my hotel. My bedroom is on the first floor and is really quite ordinary; it contains a bed, a chair, a chest of drawers and a wardrobe.

We arrived here about five o'clock and as dinner is not until 6.30 I have time to change and settle in.

The nearer dinnertime gets, the more nervous I begin to feel about going down to the dining room. I shall be all right if I have a table on my own but I do not think I could share a table with others.

There really was no need for me to worry for I do have my own table in the dining room and I feel silly for having caused myself so much ferment in thinking about this meal. One of the other tables is occupied by a young man who is also dining alone. It would be good practice for me if I could get into conversation with him. My table is between this young man's and the door so that he must pass me to leave the dining room. I have decided to wait at my table until he has finished his meal and is leaving the dining room. As he walks past me I rise and say to him, 'That was a nice meal.'

'Yes, the hotel food is quite good. Are you on holiday?'

'No, I have come to work in London. Have you been here long?'

'No. Like you I am working here for a short time.' We have left the dining room and are standing in the hotel foyer.

'I have arrived only today. I don't know London, as I have never been here before. I am staying here at the hotel for a while. What is there to do in the evening?'

'Nothing much in the hotel. I have been here a week. I would be glad to show you around the district a little if you would like that.'

'That is kind of you. I would enjoy that.' We exchange names and arrange to meet again in the lobby in ten minutes.

I learned from our brief association this evening that Tim is a little older than I am. He has a mop of black hair and he comes from Bradford. He took me all around the district and seemed to accept me very well. When we parted late this evening it was as though we had been friends for years. It is a marvel to me that I could leave home this morning, settle into a new situation and make a friend so quickly. The shame is that I cannot share the excitement I feel. I'm not sure that

100

anyone can possibly understand what it has been like for me to be released from the bonds of almost complete non-communication to this sort of freedom and the stimulation of being understood, even by strangers.

I go to sleep thinking that tomorrow may be the first day of a new life, for having met Tim and talked with him without too many misunderstandings or problems has given me huge confidence at just the right time. I know that my job is going to offer me an opportunity to grow and to build on my potential as never before.

Going down to breakfast this morning is not the ordeal that dinner was yesterday. I am no longer apprehensive or worried about the dining room. There are not many people having breakfast. It is a little early but I am keen to get to work. Tim is approaching my table.

'Good morning, Alan. Did you sleep well?'

'Good morning, Tim. Yes, thank you. Did you?'

'Yes. Do you mind if I join you? There is no need for us to sit separately.'

I feel panic rise as I wonder how Tim is going to take my style of eating. Because of my shaky hands, instead of raising the food to my mouth I have to bring my mouth down to meet my hand; my chewing process is unusual too, but I cannot say no to Tim. That would be most impolite. I must be sociable, it is part of my new self.

'Yes, Tim, please do join me.'

If only my family could see me now. What would they say? All the fuss they made about me coming to London, and not only have I made a friend, but Tim is actually asking me if I would like to go with him to the theatre tonight. He is seeking my companionship. What a thrill that is. Tim was a complete stranger yesterday and he can't have found it too embarrassing to talk to me otherwise he wouldn't be inviting me to go out with him this evening.

Miss Partridge is waiting for me as I arrive early at the office and we get down to work straightaway. I have less than three weeks to find out all I can about the many associations which care for the handicapped and I have to make arrangements for a number of visitors who will be coming to

101

England in the next few months. I have lots of reading to do and many letters to send out about forthcoming visitors. I have the help of a secretary called Helen, and I learn more from her than from anyone else. She organizes me, makes all my appointments and advises me on the layout and structure of my letters. If it were not for Helen I think I would make a shambles of the administrative side of the job.

One of my concerns, as always, is my style of eating. I will have to entertain overseas visitors and I am worried about my physical appearance at mealtimes. At the end of my first week I approach Miss Partridge about this. She has been friendly and helpful throughout my first week and she now invites me to lunch. We go to a restaurant which is rather classy and I am a little confused by all the elegance. However, I remember being taught to start at the outside with the cutlery and work towards the plate. I even manage a glass of wine without too much difficulty. I receive nothing but praise from Miss Partridge at the end of the meal.

'I think you got that meal out of me under false pretences, Alan. Your eating is quite acceptable, like everything else you do. You have no need to be concerned. Look, there is no mess and I didn't help you at all. Anyone who knew your difficulties would admire the way in which you cope. You have been watched closely all this week at the office and everyone is impressed. We are convinced that we got the right man for the job. So don't think too much about what you call problems; we are happy to have you with us and we like you just the way you are.'

I don't know how to respond to such a speech for I am embarrassed, but it is good to know that my employers approve of me.

Tim and I are dining out tonight. We fancy a change from the hotel. We have a drink in the bar before we leave the hotel. This evening it is my treat and while I cannot afford anything really grand I would like to go to a restaurant which has a bit of style. Since I'm in charge this evening, I act with confidence but as I am speaking to the waiter to order the food, he puts his ear down on a level with my mouth. This looks most peculiar but maybe he is having

102

difficulty in understanding what I am saying and is trying to listen to me more closely. I am wrong. He has stopped me in mid-sentence and is saying, 'You're drunk. I am sorry, we cannot serve you.'

Tim and I are looking at each other in disbelief, for we have only had one drink. Tim is more shocked than I am.

'I am sorry, sir, I am not drunk. I do have a speech impediment and I have had just one drink, but I am certainly not drunk,' I reply.

'I cannot serve you. Kindly leave.'

Tim is looking most embarrassed and the other diners are able to hear the waiter's accusations.

'You have made a mistake. You are quite wrong, my friend and I are not drunk and we would like to order a meal.'

'No, sir, he is drunk. We do not serve drunks in here. Would you kindly leave the restaurant.'

We could argue forever but it is better that we leave. We have found another restaurant further along the road and we have been served with our meal without any trouble. Tim is horrified about the incident in the first restaurant. I relate a few more incidents from my past and I prove my point when we are leaving the restaurant, by ringing for a taxi from a phone box. Five minutes after I have ordered the cab, Tim is ringing the same taxi firm to order one in his name. I know that the car which I have ordered will not arrive. Sure enough, Tim's is here. Tim has asked the driver to wait and is ringing to ask what happened to the taxi which I ordered.

'No taxi booked in the name of Counsell.'

'But I stood here with him and heard him book it.'

'I remember some drunk ringing in just before you rang but we never send a taxi if we know the customer is drunk.'

Tim and I have a much closer relationship after these two incidents and now that we know each other better I am telling him some of the feelings I had before my first meal in the hotel. Tim can understand how I felt and see why my confidence is sometimes shaky, after seeing the two episodes tonight but he says that he is amazed at the way I manage.

After nearly three weeks in London I am now on my way home. I will not arrive until late tonight but as it is Thursday my father will be working in the bakehouse. As I expected, mother has remained up with father and they are soaking up the stories which I am relating about my escapades in the big city.

My return is an excuse for a family gathering and once again I enjoy the safety of their presence. Here I feel no competition or stress, but a calmness; the strain of the past three weeks is gone. This time at home is a chance to refresh myself amongst familiar faces and surroundings.

Eileen is visiting me and is telling me of a boyfriend she has found. I do not know if I approve or not; I am not used to Eileen swooning over boys and I am hoping she is not going to get hurt. I will be meeting the boyfriend when I go to tea this afternoon with her family.

I am not impressed and neither are Eileen's parents. The chap seems slightly dopey and does not seem to be on our wavelength, but I am sure Eileen knows him better than I do. Maybe he is different when they are alone.

It is rather early in the morning for Eileen to be visiting. I am still in bed and have to rise quickly.

'To what do I owe this early call?'

'I want to know what you thought about Gordon. He liked you; he said that I had described you all wrong and made him think you were much worse than you are. I think you impressed him.'

'That's nice to know. How long have you known him?'

'We have been going out together for about five weeks now.'

'How serious are you? I don't want you to get hurt.'

'I think we are both serious. I don't think Gordon would hurt me.'

'Eileen, when you say serious, you're not thinking of marriage, are you?'

'Yes, it is a possibility.'

'Eileen, do be careful.'

'Why? What makes you say that?'

'Look, I don't know Gordon at all so I cannot really judge.

104

Just make sure he is right for you before you commit yourself.'

'I will. Didn't you like him?'

'We know each other too well not to be honest with each other. He seems to be rather dull and dim to me. Then again, I don't know him and he may grow on me with time.'

'Mum and dad don't like him either. I understand him. He comes from a very good family. Lots of money. His younger brother is very clever and Gordon feels an outcast. He can't compete with his family. He is not as bright as they are and so he feels inadequate and has problems with people socially. I thought you might understand better than most.' Eileen is understandably affronted and defensive.

'Eileen, give me a chance. I don't know him yet, do I? All that matters to me is that you are happy. We have been through all this before. We are like brother and sister and we both know that it would have been wrong to marry each other. We don't have that kind of feeling, but I am still very concerned about what you do in your life.'

'Yes, I know all that, and that's why it is important to me that you like Gordon.'

'I'll have to try to get to know him.'

Eileen seems to go home feeling that I am against her friendship with Gordon, and she may be right. I am worried by the impression he gave yesterday.

I feel restless thinking about all this, and that Eileen must be upset by the things which I said about Gordon, so I am visiting her in her home early on Sunday morning. We are continuing our conversation about Gordon and about the future. Suddenly we notice the time. Eileen sings in a church choir and unless she leaves now she will be late. I go along with her but when we arrive at the church the service has already begun.

'Look, Alan, you go along in. I can't walk through the congregation and into the choir with everyone watching. I'll go through the schoolroom and join the choir from behind — that way I'll be less conspicuous.'

I take a seat at the back of the church and watch for Eileen's appearance. Soon I see the door behind the choir

105

open a little way; two men from the choir pull the piano forward and Eileen appears as the door opens wider. Everyone in the church is aware that Eileen is late for church this morning. There isn't room for her to get through the door because of the piano near the door. A normal-sized person could have done it but Eileen is so much bigger than average. She has the ability to laugh at incidents like this and makes everyone else laugh with her. She does not seem at all embarrassed, or if she is she covers it well.

Walking through town this morning I meet Uncle Tom and Aunty Edith, who are virtually strangers to me. We have quite a long conversation and they are interested in the work I am doing in London. They have invited me to tea but as I must be back in London tomorrow, I have to decline. I say I will call on them when I am next home.

I leave this afternoon because I have to be at London airport by 10.30 tomorrow morning to meet my first two visitors.

Helen is with me at the airport because the two people we are meeting will arrive on separate flights, one half an hour after the other, and we do not want to leave the first one alone while we meet the second one.

An Israeli doctor is the first to arrive and we have no problem in making contact with him as he recognizes the badges which Helen and I are wearing. He is a small, olive-skinned man with dark wavy hair and looks as if he is in his early thirties. As we have a short while to wait for our next visitor, the doctor suggests that we sit in the café. His confidence and assurance make me feel inferior. He has a commanding personality and he is almost flirting with Helen. He is chatty and is telling us about his recent visit to America, already comparing our country to the United States. I am interested to learn about the Israeli system for the handicapped. If parents have a handicapped child, the whole family are given a house in a special village. These villages have many such children and their parents, sisters and brothers have common problems and can talk about them with people who understand. It sounds like a good system and I can see such a method allowing the handicapped to become more involved in the community and less isolated through general social ignorance. The doctor seems keen on his own country's practices and impressed by what he saw in America, but appears critical of what he has heard so far about England.

We have been in the café for about half an hour and it is time to meet our second visitor. Helen is reluctant to be left alone with the doctor so she is going to meet the flight from Russia.

Our Russian friend is a tall, fair man with broad shoulders and a very friendly smile. He is rather different from the Israeli visitor. His English is not so good but I can understand him if I listen carefully and he is pleasant company.

Our journey back to London is by train; the doctor from Israel has grumbled all the way and says that he will hire a car tomorrow. The arrangements for the visits to the various establishments around England have all been made and I have worked out our travelling details so that we are using trains and being met at the different stations by cars from the places we are to visit. If this man hires a car it means having to replan the whole of the next two weeks.

We have finally arrived at our hotel in London and the two visitors have been shown to their rooms. I make a point of showing them where my room is in case they need to make contact with me. While the men are unpacking and settling in I go to my room to read for a while. . . . The Israeli doctor is already knocking on my door to ask again about hiring a car. I feel I ought to make a stand. I don't like his attitude and if I don't assert myself now I can see he will muddle all my plans.

'Doctor, you will not need a car. I intend to give you details of your visit at teatime and you will see how busy we are going to be over the next two weeks. Everything has been arranged for us to travel by train and we are going to have very few days when we are not travelling, so you will not need a car.'

'I want to enjoy myself while I am here and I can do that better if I have a car.'

'Very well, doctor, but could we discuss this over tea with our other visitor because it affects him too?'

107

'What time is tea? I suppose there might be a facility in the hotel for hiring a car. I could make inquiries.'

'I would like you to leave the question of a car until after tea, if you don't mind.'

When we all sit down together I explain the itinerary and stress that the governments of Israel and Russia are paying for this visit to England and that all the plans and details of the next two weeks have been sent to the respective government departments. I am asking what the doctor meant when he was speaking to me earlier about having a good time. I am concerned, as the escort, that I do the right things. On the schedule which I have been given it looks as though the next two weeks will be spent in visits and study rather than enjoyment. The Russian visitor agrees that he was aware that the next twelve days were to be spent working and that he has arranged to spend time in England after the official tour is over to do his own sightseeing. After this conversation there is no more mention of a car and I feel I have made my point without offending my guests.

Miss Partridge has joined us for dinner and to reinforce my position I mention to her while we are eating that the doctor is thinking of hiring a car. I dare say I sound rather bumptious but I am anxious that my responsibilities should not be undermined so early in my work. Miss Partridge is reiterating what I said during tea and I think ideas of a good time have left the doctor's mind.

The next two weeks go smoothly. We travel around visiting the different centres and I explain their function. We meet dozens of people; I am amazed at myself, for with very little effort I find I can get along with strangers quite well. Of course most people we meet are used to people with physical impediments and difficulties.

The visitor from Russia has proved to be the gentleman he seemed when we first met. I really admire his manners and tact and I think he must he pleased with my efforts during his visit to England for as we part he hands me an envelope containing ten pounds and says that it is for my help. When I check at the office after the tour I receive encouragement from all concerned. I feel elated, but it is still hard for me to adjust to praise and approval.

My next assignment is in three weeks' time, when I have to meet a group from Brazil, so I am going to spend these weeks claiming unemployment benefit while living with my parents.

My family gather round and want to hear all about my experiences at work. I realize as I am speaking that I have done things, visited places and even eaten food which they have sometimes never even heard of, let alone experienced. My home and life in Blackburn seem very dowdy to me now. The warmth of my family is something which I will always cherish, but living away from them for the past few weeks has changed my standards and I do not see why my home should not be a little grander than it is. These thoughts are received stiffly, especially by my mother. I am told that I am getting ideas above my station. I invite mother and father to dine with me one evening at a hotel in town but they both decline, saying 'That would be too posh for us.'

The last time I was home I had an invitation to visit Uncle Tom and Aunty Edith, so I am knocking on their door hoping they don't mind me calling without having made an arrangement.

'Alan, this is a surprise. Come in.'

We make easy conversation, they seem interested in my work in London and we have a lot to talk about. I have only met these relatives fleetingly throughout my life and I am surprised at the rapport we have; they seem very intelligent and kind. I feel a real affinity towards Uncle Tom. I have stayed longer than I intended and realize that they may not have eaten. I rise from my seat and prepare to say goodbye but I am invited to stay to supper.

We have sat down to our meal and uncle says to aunty, 'Will you ask a blessing?'

We bow our heads and aunty says grace but it is not the ordinary kind of grace; it seems to be made up of her own words. I notice too that they do not serve coffee with their meal.

It is nine o'clock and while they are washing up in the

kitchen, I think it might be a nice gesture if I go and bring in a bottle of wine. I shout to them, 'Would you like some wine or something? I noticed there is an off-licence round the corner.'

'No, thank you, Alan. We don't drink any alcohol.'

This is a surprise to me for they have a reputation within the family for being quite fond of a drop. Uncle Tom appears from the kitchen. 'We no longer drink, Alan. We have joined the Mormon Church, which is the nickname for the Church of Jesus Christ of Latter-day Saints.'

I have never heard of the Mormon Church so Uncle Tom is soon explaining about it. We have talked until the early hours of the morning, and as I am leaving aunty produces a bag of books about their religion which she thinks I may like to read.

My visit to Uncle Tom's has left me with an appetite for further talks. I want to see more of him. I visit several times during my period at home and I am impressed by the way that both aunt and uncle live their religion. I have met some of their friends from their church as well and while I find their ideas rather extreme, they do seem to be concerned for each other. My experience of religion has been confined to attendance now and again at Church of England services with Aunty Elsie, and I have not become involved in deep or doctrinaire conversations about Christianity. Through meeting Uncle Tom regularly I have begun to think about religion. Uncle Tom and I have had long discussions about dogma, doctrine and deity. These have been fascinating and complex. It is not that I do not believe in God, it is just that I have several questions which no one has ever answered. Not that I have specifically asked them of anyone, but discussions and church sermons have not yet begun to answer my own questionings. Uncle Tom is not a high churchman but he makes his religion sound worthwhile. He would like me to meet the missionaries from his church, but as I only have two days before I return to London I feel that that can wait.

Here I am in London again, at Heathrow, waiting for the party from Brazil. Their interpreter is not very happy to

110

meet me, and refuses to believe that I am the group's guide. He has to ring the office to make sure that I really am the person sent to meet them. I feel worried; this is only my second tour and I am afraid that my bosses might begin to think I can't handle the job when they hear of this misunderstanding with the Brazilians. I can't say I blame them, for on entering a foreign country it must be a surprise to meet someone who looks and talks like me.

After the official tour, the Brazilian party remain in London for a bit of a holiday and ask if I might stay with them as their guide. They are even offering to pay all my expenses. I am relieved to take this as an indication that I have, after all, been a successful escort.

One of the highlights of my time spent with the party from Brazil is a visit to the Festival Hall restaurant; the meal is the most sophisticated and expensive I could have imagined. I now love to eat out in grand surroundings. I enjoy this occasion so much that I take a menu to show my family. When they see the menu, they seem to realize – not without some misgivings – that when I am away from them I am enjoying a different life style. I like to cook, and being unemployed gives me plenty of time to do so. Being away from home has given me experience of different cuisines and I enjoy spending long hours in my mother's kitchen preparing a meal and making the table look nice with flowers and wine. This is not really appreciated by my family, who say I am getting too posh. I must admit that I now find myself hoping that I can move on to a better way of life where there is time for niceties and stylish surroundings.

My view of the world has expanded and I have ambitions to achieve a little more than Alker Street, Blackburn, can offer. For all this grand thinking, however, I would hate to ostracize myself from my family and their affections. My new ideas are related to my self-image: people tend to look down upon me because of my handicap and I sometimes think that I am treated as a second-rate citizen. If I could raise my standards and develop a little grandness myself, I have a feeling that people's attitude towards me might be changed.

At home between tours I have met the Mormon missionaries and have been to meetings in their church. I am impressed by their concern for each other; they create a warm atmosphere when they are together and while their thinking is unconventional compared with other Churches, I am becoming more and more attracted to it. I have talked with the missionaries many times and have discussed many dilemmas and problems. The missionaries always have an answer which seems logical and acceptable. The Mormon Church does not have any paid ministry and I find the Sunday sermons that are preached by the members themselves, stimulating and informative.

My family think that I have gone stark raving mad and mother relates stories from her earlier life about incidents in which Mormons in black hats came and carried off young girls. Apparently anyone who joins the Mormons is eccentric, or barmy. I do not want to be classed in either of these categories and consider very carefully whether I ought to continue my association with the Mormons. In the end I must follow my instincts and join the Church.

Although my family try to talk me out of being baptized into the Church (membership is by baptism by immersion), I consider that I have found something which is of value.

It is not just a religious appeal: the social aspects of the Church attract me as well. They have a Relief Society which teaches the women how to become better homemakers, mothers and wives. They have a Mutual Improvement Association where the youth are taught culture and doctrine and are tutored into becoming better citizens. The vastness of the Church and the organization of its many facets impresses me.

I have nevertheless been deeply affected by the family's views and I am reluctant to tell anyone of my beliefs in case they think I am a nutcase. After a few months of membership I am asked to speak at a Sunday meeting; this kind of participation in the Church and the fact that I meet so many members from other towns is giving me more confidence towards my life in general.

As a Mormon I am told by the leader of the Church, a prophet of God, that I should not drink tea or coffee, not smoke tobacco and not take alcohol, as these are stimulants and bad for our bodies. This is a law called 'the word of wisdom' and is a requirement of membership of the Church. I am sure that living this law is responsible for my feeling physically better. Since the years when I had a problem with alcohol I have been afraid that I might go back to drinking heavily, but having the Church to support me I feel less vulnerable.

6

My contract as an escort has ended after eighteen months and once again I am unemployed. During the course of my work and travels I have come into contact with the Spastics Society. I approach it for work and am given an appointment to see someone from the employment department. She is unable to help me permanently but asks me to work as a housefather for two weeks on an assessment course.

This is being held at a school in Ivybridge, near Plymouth. The purpose of the course is to assess the abilities of teenage spastics for possible future employment. My job is to help the male students with their washing and dressing and to supervise in the dormitories. I also give them assessment tests when required. There are thirty-four spastic people on the course and I am horrified when I realize that I am, for most social intents and purposes, classed in the same category as they are. I cannot identify with them; they seem much more handicapped than I. I can see why the word spastic is such an emotive one. Some of these people have perpetually contorting features and walk around in horribly awkward and misshapen postures. They seem to be socially immature too, compared with other people of their age. It is very difficult to come to terms with the fact that the label 'spastic' applies to me as well as to the people here.

After the course I am invited to help on another in Bexhill-on-Sea, which makes me feel that I did the right things on the first course. I am asked to do many more courses and become fascinated by this work.

Blackburn has a branch of the Spastics Society and I have become slightly involved with it. I have been asked to give a

114

talk to the local Rotary Club on its behalf. My talk is entitled 'What is a spastic?' Through the experience of speaking in the Mormon church regularly I am not as nervous as I used to be about talking in public. However the room to which I have been taken is laid out for a meal and I think I must be in the wrong place. When I ask for the secretary I discover to my horror and embarrassment that I *am* in the right room and that I will speak after a meal at which I am expected to sit at the top table. How am I supposed to relax when I feel every eye in the room is upon me? The only mishap I have while eating is with my peas; I spill them all over the table. Not just one or two, not just one forkful, but several forkfuls. Each time I take a load of peas to my mouth they scatter all over the table because my hand is shaking so much. I am increasingly nervous, and to make matters worse the chair and table are not at a convenient height for me.

I get up to give my talk and have the idea that I can make use of the pea incident to introduce my topic. 'Ladies and gentlemen, I am sure that you all noticed that my peas went all over the table when I was eating. I am now going to tell you why.'

I proceed to give my talk as I had planned it and at the end of the meeting I am asked by a number of people if I had spilled the peas on purpose to give my talk more impact. I am surprised and a bit dismayed to realize that some people even here, at a sympathetic gathering, are ready to believe that I would do such a thing deliberately.

I have been working on an assessment course in Selly Oak in Birmingham and now, at the end of the course, I am taking twelve spastics to catch a train at New Street station. The roads are busier than we expected and we are stuck in a traffic jam. It is worrying because we have not much time before the train is due to leave. We have finally arrived at the station with three minutes to spare. All the students are slow moving because of their handicap and there is nowhere to park. I leap from the vehicle, leaving the party to wonder what I am up to, rush on to the platform and approach the guard of the London train just as he is about to signal it to

115

go. After I have explained the situation the guard agrees to have the train wait until all the students are on board. To make the proceedings quicker I have asked the driver of our minibus to put the luggage in a pile on the platform while I help the students to board the train. The bus driver is anxious because he is badly parked and is afraid he might be fined.

I am now waving the party off, after loading all their cases on the by now very late train. What an effort it took to get them all on board. I am feeling very shaky, almost exhausted. As I am standing waving to the students as the train slowly pulls out I can see, to my horror, that I have forgotten to load a suitcase. My last ounce of energy is spent in running with the suitcase down the platform after the train, shouting to the students as loudly as I can for them to open the window of their compartment. I manage to throw the case into the train just as it gathers speed. The moment I have let go of the case I can feel a hand on my shoulder and hear a voice in my ear.

'Oi, that's my case!'

I turn to see an obviously dismayed woman who is becoming even more distressed as she grows aware of my jumbled speech and shaking body. She is misinterpreting my words as I try to explain the situation to her and is now backing away from me. As we pass the crowds of people waiting on the platform she repeats to each person, 'He has thrown my case on that train!'

Someone has sent for the police and they ask where I am from. They assume I am from the local subnormality hospital and are treating me like a lunatic. I am too exhausted and frightened to assert myself and have to resort to anger. I ask the police to find a witness on the platform who might have seen the whole thing. This seems the worst situation I can ever remember. I am accused of a crime and the police are aggressive with me. Luckily, however, they have found some people who saw the whole incident. The driver of the minibus has also appeared and the police are willing to accept his word as he vouches for me and my sanity. The police are most helpful and apologetic, now that

116

they realize I am neither mad nor drunk, and as I relax they are better able to understand me.

The unfortunate owner of the luggage had apparently come on to the platform and put down her case while she went for a cup of coffee. She placed her bag where my pile of cases had been and I did not see her.

I think the constable is trying to cheer me up when he says to her, 'Madam, where are you travelling to?'

'I am going to Scotland.'

'Well you had better go via London and pick your case up on the way.'

Although this incident may be amusing in retrospect, I do feel for the woman concerned. I can't imagine how alarmed she must have felt when she was confronted by my shaking body and distorted features.

When I return home I find that my father has been taken ill again. He was gassed in the First World War and this affected his heart and lungs. He is now having heart attacks and each time the family are called to his bedside.

Each time he comes round and sees us there he greets us with the same words. 'What the hell are you lot standing there for? Go away, you make me feel worse than I really am. I'm not going to die with you lot looking on.'

We know that he is much worse than he likes to admit, but he always seems to rally after a few days' rest and refuses to be treated like an invalid.

While I am at home between temporary jobs I become restless and dissatisfied again. I realize that I need a permanent job for my own self-respect and stability. I am sure that the fact that Eileen has married Gordon has something to do with my present mood. It is not that *I* want to be married yet, but it may be that I see Eileen's marriage as progress in her life and I don't feel I am making this kind of advance in mine.

It is a wonder that Eileen and I have remained friends because I still don't approve of Gordon and have told her so many times. Eileen needed lots of support before her wedding as she wanted to lose a great deal of weight. She had an incentive because of her wedding dress; she managed to lose eight stone and looked terrific on her wedding day.

In one of the local evening papers there is an advertisement for student nurses at one of the local psychiatric hospitals. Although I doubt my chances, I am going to telephone and make inquiries.

I have been connected to the chief male nurse at the hospital and I am explaining about myself. He seems interested in my previous work and is asking if I will go and see him at the hospital tomorrow.

What a beautiful drive this is. It is overhung with trees and makes a shaded walk. The grounds look well cared for, not a bit as I had imagined them to be. I am pleasantly surprised, as I had visions of something resembling a penal establishment.

The chief male nurse is taking me round the hospital and is telling me about the role and duties of a student nurse. I would spend three months in nursing school and three months on the ward, then back to nursing school, and so on for three years. If I passed my final examinations at the end of three years I would then be a registered mental nurse. The patients at the hospital are all mentally subnormal. Many of the patients, although adult, function as a young child would. I would be involved in the care of these patients rather as a father or mother might be. The patients are not sick in the physical sense, so the nursing isn't the kind one would find in a general hospital. It involves satisfying the patients' daily needs. I would be involved in feeding those patients who could not manage it by themselves, in washing, shaving, and bathing them. Some of the patients are on drug therapy and as a student I would learn how to administer drugs. I will also be introduced to the other therapies practised in the hospital.

The chief male nurse makes it sound interesting and any doubts that I have about my ability to do the work are dispelled by the offer of a place in nursing school providing that I can pass the entrance examination. There is a chance that I could have a permanent job at last; even though I am a little bothered about some aspects of the work, I am hopeful that I will overcome new problems as I have in the past.

Many of the 'higher graded' patients in the hospital are

118

here through court orders and are labelled as psychopaths. These are people who have emotional disturbances and don't really have much respect for other people or their property. Some of these psychopaths are also sexual offenders, often rather aggressive generally.

The nursing tutor has interviewed me and says he would be willing to have me as a student nurse; I must understand, though, that continuous assessment is a part of the course and if at any time I get a bad report I can be put back in the course, put to work as a nursing auxiliary or sacked. When I am given the examination papers I am not given a time limit, luckily, and I am allowed to take the exam in a room on my own. This helps enormously, taking away a great deal of the tension I would feel if I had to work against the clock with other people around me. This is the first conventional examination I have passed in my life, and I don't feel that too many allowances were made for me. I wonder how I would have done in my eleven-plus if I had been given my own time? I am grateful to the nursing tutor for making the proceedings so relaxed.

I look forward to starting my job at the hospital. I have to wait about six weeks until the next intake at the nursing school.

My first three months with the hospital have been spent in nursing school where we have had lectures and demonstrations on the types of patients and their care. Now I am working on the wards it is quite different. The patients don't really know what to make of me as they are not used to seeing a handicapped person wearing a nurse's uniform. Initially some of the less subnormal patients thought that I was one of them who had gone over to the other side! After a few weeks they seem to accept and even trust me enough to share their secrets with me. Many of the patients have severe speech problems and they need time and patience when they are trying to communicate. Unfortunately the staff–patient ratio is about one to twenty and there isn't always enough time to listen. I feel an empathy with these patients but I am always getting behind in my work and chastised by the charge nurse for spending too much time with these patients.

I remember very well what it was like trying to tell someone something and not being able to get through. I like to think that I have a special rapport with some of the patients. Certainly the phrase 'There but for the grace of God go I' runs through my mind quite often ... I think of the time when I had to face a tribunal at the time when my sanity was questioned. I try to show a lot of patience and sympathy with most of the patients and feel that they respect me for it. I only wish I had more time to give to them.

It is very different working on the wards after nursing school. There I felt relaxed, I didn't feel threatened in any way and I coped quite well. But here on the wards there are many older, trained staff who treat me as they would a patient. I can well see that these people will need time to adjust – they are used to seeing the likes of me as patients rather than colleagues. Even though I am often miserable I am not ready to give up as I feel I have an opportunity to show some of the people who work at the hospital that not all spastic people are mentally subnormal.

Being the only spastic nurse in the hospital my progress is monitored with interest by the medical superintendent. He wants to know about any problems I encounter and I find his interest encouraging. The value of this relationship is proved to me when one day I am struck by a charge nurse for not obeying his orders.

It is the practice of the ward to which I have been posted to feed the 'low grade' patients (who are unable to feed themselves) with their entire lunch mixed together on one plate. That is, meat, gravy, vegetables, pudding and custard all roughly blended together in one revolting mess. I refuse to do this for a number of reasons. I think everyone has a right to dignity, and giving a human being pig swill is not dignified. I once had to be fed and it can be a terrifying experience. Sometimes I would feel as though I was drowning when the food was pushed quickly into my mouth in big spoonfuls. I also believe that choice can be an aid to education and that choice can begin with food. I always ask my patients what they would like me to put into their mouths next. Today the charge nurse asked if I would feed the patients his way as it is quicker. I refused. The charge nurse did not argue, but clumped me behind the ears as he does many patients on his ward. He swears at me in front of the patients. I feel I should make an issue out of this, both for my sake and for the sake of the patients.

My complaint should have gone to the chief male nurse's office but I know it will have more impact if I go direct to the medical superintendent. He is horrified to hear that I have been assaulted but ironically he does not seem too concerned about the main issue, the way in which the patients are fed. He has sent for the chief male nurse and the nursing tutor and is asking me to repeat my story. They both seem annoyed at the incident and the chief male nurse is asking me, 'Why didn't you come to see me?'

'I am sorry. I was so upset. I came to the first person I thought of.'

Now the nursing tutor is questioning me as though he disbelieves my story. 'I don't understand why he hit you.'

'He hit me because I refused to mix a patient's entire lunch together all on one plate.'

'Are you saying that you refused to feed a patient?'

'No, I'm not saying that. I am saying that I like to show patients some dignity when I am feeding them. I like them to choose what goes into their mouth. I will not mix their meat and vegetables with their pudding and shovel it in.'

'Are you aware of what you are saying. It sounds to me as though you are accusing a charge nurse of neglect.'

'I'm only saying what happened. I am not being treated like a schoolboy and banged around the head and I am certainly not feeding patients as though they were pigs receiving swill.'

The conversation goes on and I am afraid that I become rather heated. Eventually the three men get to the real point and discuss the manner in which the patients are fed on certain wards. It is obvious to me that they are totally unaware of some things which go on in the hospital.

The medical superintendent is thanking me for bringing the incident to his notice and the three of us are dismissed from his office. Afterwards the chief male nurse has a different attitude. He is telling me in no uncertain terms that I was wrong to approach the medical superintendent. I am also told that as a student nurse I should never criticize a charge nurse.

The chief male nurse has sent for the charge nurse who enters the office defensively, looking at me and saying, 'Where the hell have you been?'

The charge nurse is told of my accusations and is denying the incident. He is also saying that he is officially reporting me for leaving the ward without permission while I was on duty.

Luckily my story is believed and disciplinary action is being taken against the charge nurse for his assault on me.

I am sent for by the nursing tutor and the professional code of practice is spelled out to me. I am accused of doing two things wrong. I should have taken my complaint to the chief male nurse and I should not have walked out of the ward whilst I was on duty. I am not arguing with the tutor, I am merely asking for my union representative to be present for the rest of the conversation. I am dismissed from the tutor's room and told to return to my work.

The hospital is buzzing with the scandal and there are, of course, two sides: those who support me and those who support the charge nurse.

There is a new ward rota up this morning, which is not expected as we were only assigned to our current wards a week ago and that rota was supposed to last three months. The rest of the students feel sure that our new postings are to get me away from my present ward and from the atmosphere created by the feeding incident. I feel I should leave the hospital, but it would be so hard for me to get another job that I am prepared to live with the embarrassment for a while.

There is a memo waiting for me at my new ward from the medical superintendent asking me to go and see him. Everyone has their own ideas as to what the superintendent wants me for. The majority are sure that I am going to be sacked or professionally reprimanded.

The meeting is not at all unpleasant. It is just to tell me

that the medical superintendent has ordered a change of wards and that each charge nurse is to receive a directive about feeding. He does not want to see a complete meal being mixed together for any patient. The practice has to stop. He is also saying that I must come to him with any problem that I may have; even though I have told him of my meetings with the chief male nurse and the nursing tutor he insists that if I would rather talk to him then I must feel free to do so.

The ward that I am now on is very different from my last ward and the charge nurse is much better to work with. He teaches me all kinds of things and never insists that I do anything which I do not agree with. We have constructive theoretical discussions, and to my surprise I am allowed to put one of my theories into practice.

There are seventy patients on the ward and often only three or four members of staff. Many of the patients on this ward are aggressive low-grades who are unpredictable in their behaviour. They assault each other and tear each other's clothing. They fight and sometimes cause serious harm to one another. They destroy the ward furniture and members of staff are attacked regularly. One needs eyes at the back of one's head. Thus the main occupation of the nursing staff is observation, and many times it is regrettably necessary to tie a patient to a chair while a nurse has to leave the room or deal with some emergency. We all hate to do this but we are so short of staff; we are not being knowingly cruel, we are trying to protect the patients from one another and sometimes from causing themselves harm.

There are twelve patients on the ward who are more intelligent than the rest and they are deployed as helpers. Indeed, they work as hard as the staff. While these patients can be unpredictable, they are usually helpful and work tirelessly. Even so they are told what to wear, when to eat, when to take a bath and even often when to go to the toilet. They seldom have the opportunity to make any decisions for themselves. They are not given any praise or payment for their work, yet often they work from early morning until late in the evening. I am interested in this group of patients and

123

suggest that if they were given a few constructive privileges they might respond favourably. I also suggest that some of these higher-grade patients might be able to return to normal society one day and that maybe we could be helping them to prepare for this. This view is not shared by many people at the hospital at the time.

My ideas have obviously been discussed by the chief male nurse and the charge nurse for I have been assigned a dormitory for the twelve patients who help on the ward. I would like these higher-grade patients to have a better self-image and to be more aware of their own potential. They currently mingle with the worst patients in the hospital and they are beginning to identify with them rather than seeing their own true worth. Henceforth, the patients are going to choose what they wear themselves and are going to do their own personal washing, with the hope that this will help them to have more pride in their appearance. Their meals will be eaten in their own dormitory after they have finished helping to feed the rest of the patients; at all mealtimes they will set a table and eat like civilized humans. They will be able to take a bath when they want and once a week they are to be allowed to use the ward kitchen to cook themselves an evening meal. All the activities of the residents in my new dormitory are being recorded and at the end of three months there is to be a meeting of the top people in the hospital to discuss the project and its future.

It has taken time for the boys to settle in their dormitory. They could not get used to the new system at first, but now, I think, they work even harder on the ward and they have far fewer grumbles than they used to. They meet me each lunchtime and talk about their problems and their feelings; we are developing quite a relationship. Sometimes the charge nurse will join us for our daily meetings. He is encouraging and full of enthusiasm.

The dormitory is decorated with the boys' own choice of pictures and we even have a few books. Clothing cupboards are kept tidy and the patients are encouraged to keep their possessions orderly. In fact there is an all-round general improvement.

124

Praise for the success of the project goes to the charge nurse. My efforts are not acknowledged, but I don't really mind because the patients are the ones who are ultimately receiving the benefits. Privately, I revel to think that I am actually responsible for effecting so much change.

My home life is difficult because my standards have altered and I hanker for a different life style from that of my parents. I feel it would be better if I left home and found somewhere of my own. Mother and father think I am very silly when I talk about moving into a flat. They don't think I would manage and say I would be back with them within a week. I'm sure they are wrong; I have given the matter a lot of thought and I do not think I would have too many problems. However, I really want to make sure before I make the final decision; I could not bear to leave home and then return having failed.

I have found an unfurnished flat with the help of a nursing colleague. At the moment the flat is occupied by a brother and sister who are both going to be married within the next two months. I can't take the flat until they leave so at least I have time to shop around for the things I will need; it is difficult to know where to begin.

It is expensive and exhausting trying to buy all I need to set up my own home; it is particularly difficult because I have only seen the flat once and can't quite remember the size and layout of the rooms.

All the planning of the last two months has now come together to produce a home which looks cosy and modern. As I sit in my lounge on the first evening I feel proud of my home; it looks smashing. I have had all three rooms decorated and fitted with carpets, and with all my bits and pieces around me I feel I belong here. It is a marvellous feeling to sit in my very own flat for the first time. I do not know yet how I am going to manage living alone but as I know that a good many people expect me to return to my parents' home after failing, I am determined that I will deal with all the problems. I believe I will enjoy living here. I have already overcome one problem: wiring plugs. Some

of the screws are far too small for my fingers but I perse-
vered and although it took ages I managed in the end.
Similarly, screwing hooks into the window frames to take
a wire to hang nets from took a long time, but I finally
managed it.

My main ambition, the event that I am most looking
forward to, is to entertain my mother and father for a meal in
my new home. I remember that they expect me to fail at
living alone so I am sharpening my cooking and hosting skills
before I invite them; luckily, I have other visitors to practise
on. Quite soon I feel I have reached an acceptable standard,
so my parents are visiting me today for the first time. I feel
apprehensive, as I think they may find my ideas on home
decor and so on too different from theirs and may well throw
out comments about being posh or living above my station.
They can see there is no doubt that I can manage on my own
– I have been in my flat for almost two months. From what
my parents are saying, this visit has helped them a great deal;
they had been worried about what kind of place I was living
in and how I was coping on my own. They seem impressed by
my home and by the meal. They say that they had wanted to
come and see me before today but they were afraid that I
might think they were interfering.

Living on my own gives me opportunities for developing
basic social skills that were less necessary while I had mother
and father to protect me. I am finding it easier to make
friends and am becoming more outward-going. It is also good
to be able to entertain friends with no one to censor or
comment.

I like to impress my family by the things I do and the
friends I have. I suppose I want to show them that I have
changed from the helpless person they knew into an
independent young man. I am not always pleasant to my
family, because they know me far too well and they comment
on my new life. I am sometimes too protective of myself to be
polite, but I am sure that this is understood by my family.
The worst problem which I have overcome is fear. Fear of
failing, not just physically but socially. I was afraid to make
friends, I did not know how I was going to be received in the

126

community when I moved into my flat, and I feel a triumph as I realize that the fear has gone.

Tom, my younger brother, has got engaged. I have not yet met his future wife, so I have invited them to tea today. My sister is to bring them over in her car. Olive has arrived alone and there is no explanation as to why Tom and his girlfriend have not come. I have gone to a lot of trouble to prepare this meal and the fact that they have not turned up is annoying.

It is difficult to sort out my thoughts about this. It is all too easy to remember my school days, the isolation I experienced, and the comments I suffered about my handicap in the past; it is easy also to imagine that Tom has told his girlfriend about my condition and that she is too frightened to meet me. Or even, because I am a spastic, that I am beneath her interest. Thoughts like this should be repressed, for they are foolish; I realize that perhaps I am too sensitive. But past experiences are hard to overcome.

After many weeks of waiting I have met Tom's fiancée. She seems nice and although we don't get on like a house on fire, we are amicable. She has asked if I will be a groomsman at the wedding.

Already my family are making comments about there only being me left single after Tom is married. I must say that marriage seems a long way off for me, in fact pretty unlikely altogether. Actually, the topic is a bit of a sore point for me. I do want to get married but who would want me as their husband? I have been through this a thousand times in my head, but while I can say this to myself, I would be hurt to think that other people thought or said the same. I have had a few girlfriends but no one special. I did get involved on two occasions with girls who were handicapped but I feel that to marry such a person might compound both our difficulties. So now my girlfriends, as such, are all normal.

Because of those comments about me not being married and because I feel other people might be thinking that I can't get girlfriends, I am taking the most attractive girl I know to Tom's wedding. What a sensation. All my family relatives want to know who she is and are wildly interested in her. She is a weaver from Preston and I know her through the Church.

I have never had so many inquisitive invitations to tea – of course all the invitations include Barbara – but I am unpopular, as I turn them all down. Barbara and I are casual friends; we don't have the sort of relationship which would include going around to relatives for tea and being sized up.

There are not many young men of my age in the Church but I have formed a close relationship with one of them, Michael, who comes from Preston. We have got to know each other gradually over the last six months and we find that we have a great deal in common. Being a Mormon can be lonely as one's social life is restricted by not drinking and by all the meetings members have to attend. So it is good to have a close friend who shares my philosophical views as well. Michael often spends the weekend at my flat; as he has a car we are able to visit other branches of the Church and make new friends. We enjoy many other activities, and naturally enough we are both interested in girls and in finding a wife. There is an abundance of females but a dearth of males within the Mormon Church, so we find ourselves quite popular!

Michael and I talk together at great length and I am just becoming aware of how the use of language helps my thought processes. I know that many of my past problems would have seemed much easier and smaller if I had had the power of communication in my younger days. Not only was my speech affected, but because words themselves were so strange to me, the very development of my thoughts and ideas must have been affected too.

Michael and I do not confine ourselves to Church activities and we often use my flat to entertain our other friends. Tonight we went to a local dance and ended up having sixteen people back for coffee in my flat. They all stayed the night. I really have never had such fun in my life and I know this sort of thing would not be possible if I still lived with my parents.

My colleagues at the hospital have seen me with so many different girls that they now called me 'Casanova Counsell'. The hospital organizes a dinner-dance every month and I attend each of them always with a new partner. I don't have a special girlfriend as I have not yet met a girl who I can be serious about. But I do like girls' company and I feel I should try to meet as many different people as possible, so that if one day I do marry I will be better able to make the right choice.

Things are again beginning to get difficult for me at work. As a second-year student I am supposed to learn how to give injections and measure medicines, and I know that because of my poor hand control I will not be able to manage. I am going to have to give up nursing and this depresses me as I felt I could be useful in this career.

However, the medical superintendent is suggesting that I become the hospital's welfare worker. This entails dealing with social problems that the patients may have, in family matters or with the outside world. I will organize transport and travel warrants for those patients who are on parole. I will also need to organize clubs for the blind, the deaf, and the physically handicapped, as well as general groups for the interests of the patients.

After working as a welfare worker for six months I now have the chance to take a social work course at a college in Manchester. The hospital authorities will pay all my expenses and I will spend two days at college each week.

I am daunted to learn that I need O levels to gain entry to the course. At my interview I explain that I was not able to take GCE at the usual age because of physical and emotional problems, but say that if the interview panel could accept that I had studied textiles and nursing since I left school then that may prove my ability to cope with the academic content of the course. To my surprise I have been accepted.

The list of subjects to be studied on the course is impressive: economic history, the structure of the state welfare system and applied psychology, to mention only three of the subjects which interest me. I shall attend college for one year and if I successfully complete the course I will be awarded an Inservice Certificate in Social Welfare.

This is the first time I have attended a session of the course, which is at Bracken House, a part of Manchester University.

129

I feel uncomfortable as we sit in the tiered seating of a lecture theatre. We have to fill out forms and they have to be completed so quickly. I just hope that whoever reads my forms knows that I am handicapped. It looks like Chinese, I have had to write in such a hurry. I have not seen anyone I know all morning, and I wonder if the lecturers are actually expecting me in their groups because each time I have spoken I have received a funny look. At the beginning of something new it is always difficult for me to make friends; I have been mistaken so often for a mental case that I have come to expect this reaction and rather steel myself. Many people have smiled at me during the morning but I sense some bafflement behind their good will.

Every six months there is a mental health tribunal at the hospital, where different cases are reviewed. I have to make a visit to the patient's home and send a report to the tribunal. This time the patient in question comes from Liverpool and has been placed in hospital by the courts for stealing from supermarkets and shops. His records say that he is a psychopath. It is an education for me when I eventually find his family's house.

The sight of the street horrifies me. There is a mass of litter everywhere and the stench is indescribable. I happen to be fond of the patient in question and I am upset to think of him living in a place like this. I am amazed when my knock is answered and I look into the face of what can only be described as a pathetically wizened old woman. She is dressed in rags and is wearing a very shabby fur coat. The stink from the open door of the house is foul. She tells me that she is the person I am looking for, the mother of my patient, although she looks far too old to be the mother of a twenty-year-old. I announce who I am and I am invited into the house. The place is littered with bottles of every description and there are piles of rubbish everywhere. I cannot believe that this is someone's home. The table has only one leg; at the other three corners there are piles of bricks. There are no chairs, just a very old mattress on the floor, where I am invited to sit.

130

When I explain why I have come the woman becomes animated. 'You are a welfare worker? I thought you had come from the hospital. I thought you were one of the patients who had been with my son.'

'No, I thought I told you who I was when you opened the door to me.'

'No, you didn't. I thought you said you were a mate of my son's. I don't want any bloody welfare officers in my house. I don't want your sort round here.'

The woman becomes aggressive and as it is difficult to calm her, I think it is best to leave. As I get to the front door the woman calms herself enough to ask, 'Mister, before you go, do you have the price of a pint?'

It is hard to believe that the woman I have just left is the mother who is talked of with such affection by my patient. The longer I am in this job the more I realize that mothers are important to their children however inadequate they are.

My report describes the patient's home situation and recommends that the patient be placed in a local authority hostel rather than return home. But it is not considered relevant because the local authority social worker is saying that the family will be rehoused in time for the patient's release. This may solve part of the problem. But I have a gut feeling that if the patient returns to live with his mother, it will not be long before we see his return to the hospital under a court order.

It will be some time before my opinions in such cases are given much credence. I have learned to accept this, in fact I still pinch myself (or would, if my hand didn't shake), to make myself believe that I am working as a welfare officer. My job presents problems and engenders dispute, true, but they are largely the kind of disagreements that take place between equals. A few years ago the idea of someone taking my ideas seriously (and, come to that, understanding what I was saying) enough to dispute them vehemently would have been laughable. I realize that in some ways I am in a transitional phase: replacing one set of potential difficulties with a new one. Sometimes it still feels as if I've acquired the new without shifting the old....

131

7

My father has had yet another heart attack and we have all been called home. These attacks are happening even more frequently now but father refuses to give up; he is usually back at work after a short rest, despite the doctor's warning that he must take things easy. Father has a special reason for not dying: he says that he will not give up on life until he sees me married.

I wonder. I have been able to make some good relationships with girls but I doubt if anyone could stand to live with my voice and my shakes and other physical peculiarities forever. I know people have to concentrate terribly hard on my words to understand me. Anyway, I have not yet met a girl whom I feel I want to marry.

Each branch of the Mormon Church has a midweek meeting for young people. It is called the Mutual Improvement Association and I have been given the responsibility of leading the district association, which comprises seven towns. This is quite a challenge for me as it means I have to visit each of the towns, meet the leaders of each branch to give any help or advice needed, and attend their meetings. All this means that I will have to meet many new people.

As I begin my visits to the various branches I notice how differently people respond to me. I often speculate on whether people could ignore my physical handicap if only I were able to speak clearly. As people get to know me they usually come to accept me, but initially most people find it difficult not to be embarrassed by the distortions of my voice and they have trouble knowing how best to respond to me because of that. This puts a psychological pressure on me.

132

I feel that I must at all times make sure that nothing about my appearance or behaviour could seem to confirm any erroneous theories regarding my mental capacity. So I try to be as correct as possible in all other ways.

The Accrington branch, which I am visiting tonight, holds its meetings in the home of one of the members of the Church. There is a new member present; she seems terribly shy but is so charming that I feel I want to help her to overcome her timidity. In my position I am supposed to encourage people's different talents. This new member is an accomplished pianist and so I decide to ask her to play for big events. I hope this will improve her confidence and help her to overcome her reticence. Her name is Kathleen Moon and she has a beautiful smile. Her eyes are clear and innocent and she has an old-fashioned aura about her that somehow demands a second glance. Some young men, I imagine, may find her unattractive because she is so quiet and inhibited, but I find these qualities refreshing.

My current girlfriend is an art student called Jackie who lives in Preston. I see other girls sometimes but I seem to seek Jackie's company most often. She is interesting company and quite intellectual. We have been friends for many months and she is very dear to me, but I do not find I can think of the future with her.

The field of mental health is rapidly changing and I have been asked by the hospital medical superintendent if I will go on a course to train as a rehabilitation officer. He wants me to set up a unit within the hospital which will help the growing number of patients who are being discharged to live in a normal community.

After one academic year and brandishing a new certificate for the rehabilitation of the mentally sick and mentally handicapped, I return to the hospital to open the new rehabilitation unit. I have been given a prefabricated building behind the hospital and supervise the work of five other members of staff. I am responsible for the day-to-day running of the unit and also for the individual rehabilitation programme for each patient attending. These programmes

133

can be complex; we really need a psychologist but as there is none available the unit staff themselves have to assess each patient, trying to assess the particular skills that we need to teach each if they are to fit into whatever branch of society they try to go into. The biggest problem for me is in approaching prospective employers. If these patients are going to leave hospital we should be helping them to develop a work habit, and what better way to do this than to send them out to a proper job in industry where the hospital can initially supervise them? I always make my first approach by telephone and often have embarrassing moments. Sometimes people will ask who it is, and then tell me to stop mucking about and put the phone down. Others do not answer at all but simply hang up; yet others bring a colleague because they are confused by my funny voice on the line. Ultimately, though, I get through to the personnel department. I feel it is a good thing for the ordinary person to have to deal with me because in doing so I hope that in a small way I am leading employers towards accepting handicapped people better. No matter what my reception is when I first contact a firm, I persist until I get an interview. I am no longer as sensitive as I used to be and I too have been known to yell down the telephone.

Personnel managers are sometimes embarrassed when they meet me. They seem suspicious of my handicap and it is obvious that they find it difficult to accept that someone with my disadvantages can hold a responsible position. I think, though, that when these people finally come to accept me, often through my persistence, they often develop more sympathy with the cause I am working for, which is the main thing.

Kathleen, the girl from Accrington, has invited me to her twentieth birthday party and I am surprised there at her gaiety. Amongst her family she is a different person. I have taken her out on several occasions but have found her hard going. She really is so painfully shy that she finds it a strain to make any conversation at all. Our first date was to see an Elvis Presley film called *Tickle Me*, and she did not say one word all evening! We have been to several dances and she is always quiet. I don't really know why I keep seeing her as she is not my usual type of girl. But there is something about her which I find attractive. In fact it is these very quiet and dignified, almost old-fashioned manners that both perplex and enchant me.

It is Christmas. I have a hectic time with lots of parties, but I am confused because even so I cannot get Kathleen out of my mind. Seeing her so animated at her own party has changed my opinion of her. Soon I realize that I really am serious – dancing with other girls is not much fun now, and I find that part of me wants to spend more time with Kathleen, even though another part of me criticizes the quiet way she dresses, her lack of make-up, and so forth. The reason for this criticism is that I like to impress people. I like to be noticed and I like to be seen with obviously attractive women. Really, I am being very silly – I have been too busy looking at what I saw as Kathleen's faults, the way she dresses and her shyness. She also has many good points. She is intelligent and has a sound education. She has a job as a clerk and cashier and runs the office for a leading electrical retailer. Behind the shy girl is an exuberant one. We enjoy the same sort of entertainment.

I cannot go on dithering. Tonight was the final straw. Kathleen and I went to a dance and it seemed so perfectly right when we danced together, an absence of competitiveness and an inner calm.

I have always told other girlfriends at the beginning of our relationship not to take their friendship with me seriously but now I find myself saying to Kathleen, 'I think it is about time that you and I began to think seriously about each other. What do you think?'

Of course Kathleen is far too shy to answer but her nod is enough for me. The more we see of each other the less inhibited she becomes and the mutual confidence which our relationship inspires is good for us both.

Kathleen has come to dinner tonight for the first time. For some curious old-fashioned reason it does not seem right for her to be here alone with me. I do not want any speculation

135

about her visit so I have also invited Aunty May and her friend to be here as chaperones. I have never made such an arrangement before as I have not been concerned about people talking about the girls who have visited me from time to time.

We have a new medical superintendent at the hospital and he has very different ideas to the retiring one. The rehabilitation unit is being closed down because the new superintendent wants to use the building to expand the children's school and intends to use the money formerly spent on my unit on the children's education. He feels that outside agencies should be involved in the rehabilitation of our patients and that rehabilitation should take place after the patient has been released. There are a number of local authorities who have set up what are called halfway houses which attempt the same work as the unit, so he could well be right. I am not sure now what the future will hold for me.

I have got myself a new job as a therapy assistant at another psychiatric hospital. I find the work tedious and I am sure that the patients are bored too. All they do throughout the day is pack twelve screws in an envelope, or paint toy soldiers, pack them, or stick handles on to paper carrier bags; if these activities do not bore them they are allowed to pick blue paper bits from offcuts of rolls of bandages or cotton wool. I do not really get on very well at all with this work but try as I might I cannot get another job, and will have to endure until I do. I spend more time at the doctor's and claiming sickness benefit during this period than at any other time in my working life. No matter what the doctor writes on my certificate, I know that I am really suffering from boredom.

There seems to be no other option open to me but to make the best of this unsatisfactory job and compensate by having an interesting life away from the hospital.

I am becoming increasingly emotionally involved with Kathleen and find that now I view her as a prospective wife. This causes me great inner conflict. I am not sure whether Kathleen thinks of me in the same way. Have I any right to

136

ask a girl to marry me? Am I not being unrealistic? Can I really cope with all the responsibilities of marriage? Is my condition going to improve or am I going to get worse and become a millstone to a wife? I just don't know what to do. At last I have found the girl whom I want to marry but I do not know whether I ought to ask her. I suspect that she may be expecting a proposal for I have seen her constantly over the past few weeks and have treated her with a more than friendly interest, although I have conducted a very proper and decorous pursuit. I am sure that I have given indications of my intentions and she has responded favourably. We have discussed my defects and other important issues and she is still prepared to go out with me and allow me to show my affection. I feel I ought to be open about my feelings.

We are going to see a film tonight and as we are walking to the cinema I ask casually, 'What would you like me to buy you for Christmas?'

'I don't really know.'

'How do you fancy a ring?'

'A ring? I do not wear them very often.'

'I mean an engagement ring.'

Kathleen has not spoken to me all evening. I am sure that she is aware that I have asked her to marry me, but she is silent. After the film we walk home. As I am leaving her at her door, I say to her, 'I will give you a week to think about my proposal.'

It took some bottle to ask Kathleen to marry me, even though I did it in a slightly indirect way, but her silence has really upset me. I do not know whether I have shocked or offended her, and I wonder if maybe she did not like to turn me down while I was with her. I fear I have run the risk of ending our friendship completely by my proposal. If only she had said something to me, anything but this silence which I find cruel.

I am seeing her tomorrow but having given her a week to reply, I do not suppose it would be proper for me to mention the matter so soon.

Tonight we are visiting friends in Blackburn and although I have told myself that I will not talk about my proposal I

137

cannot bear the tension between us. I feel I must say something.

'I suppose you are keeping me waiting for an answer?'

'No, I can tell you now; I will marry you.'

I can't believe my ears. Kathleen is going to marry me! My excitement is indescribable and I feel great. I have a marvellous sense of satisfaction and achievement.

Since I started living alone, each evening I usually sit before the fire in my living room before going to bed, contemplating the events of the day, analysing and formulating future tactics. Tonight I feel elated. The tension has gone and I just feel pure emotion. For the first time I can admit that I am in love. It is easy to say, and I suppose that deep down I have known it all along, but now I have succeeded in winning Kathleen I can admit it to the world. I am in love. I feel special when I am with Kathleen. She makes me feel as no one else does. Just to be near her is thrilling. I feel like dancing round the room. I love Kathleen and she is going to marry me.

Why couldn't I admit my feelings to Kathleen when I asked her to marry me? I'm not surprised, now, that I got a slightly off answer to my rather offhand proposal. I have been hurt and laughed at so often in my life that now I have built a psychological barrier around myself and protect myself the whole time. I am rather secretive and do not share my thoughts and feelings for fear of ridicule or criticism. On this occasion it would have been better not to have been so cautious. But past experiences are difficult to overcome and I had to be sure that Kathleen would accept me before I could openly admit that I love her.

Of course, now that Kathleen has accepted me I am worried about how others might view her decision. I do hope people are not going to shun her because of me. I am going to have to meet Kathleen's family and relations. Her mother and younger sister I already know quite well and I get on fine with them as a friend, but having me as one of the family is quite another matter. Her father I have only met briefly on several occasions and now I realize that as Kathleen is not yet twenty-one I am going to have to ask his consent. Kathleen assures me, however, that they were all delighted with the news, so now I feel quite confident as I approach her home to ask her father's permission. Fortunately, Kathleen's father is alone and I find him easy to talk to. He is quite happy for Kathleen to marry me if that is what she wants. Kathleen also has an older brother who is a teacher and lives in Bristol. It will be some time before I meet him but I am not concerned; the others have accepted me and so I expect he will too. Kathleen takes me to meet some of her relatives and we get on all right. I cannot help but wonder just what they really are thinking; but it does not seem to worry Kathleen, so why should I let these thoughts bother me? After all, I am going to marry Kathleen, not her relatives.

The news of our engagement is received generally with varying degrees of surprise. Reactions range from ecstasy on the part of some to stupefaction on the part of others. Our closest friends receive the news with a roar of approval – it is great to have their congratulations and warm wishes.

Kathleen and I are busy with visits to relatives of mine who want to meet her. Aunty Elsie receives Kathleen into her home as though she is a queen, and is terrifically excited about our engagement. Kathleen is made to feel so welcome and comfortable in my aunty's home that she forgets her usual shyness and chatters naturally.

Of course, the news has caused a great furore at my home because no one expected it, nor have they met Kathleen. My father was the first to be told.

'Father, are you ready to die?' I said to him in greeting, as I entered the living room.

'Now what have you done? Why should I be ready to die?'

'Well, father, you have often said in the past few months that you would not die until you saw me married. I am afraid that your time is up. I am now engaged.'

'You are going to be married? I always knew you would be the death of me. Who is she? That weaver from Preston?'

'No, you have not met this one. She is called Kathleen and she lives in Accrington.'

'You've kept it a secret! Does your mother know?'

'No, mother does not know yet.'

'You had better go and tell her then; she is in the kitchen. When do we meet her? Don't worry about me dying. I am sure that I shall live to see your first baby.'

Father took the news of my forthcoming marriage very calmly but his excitement showed when I returned from the kitchen. He had already been out and told the news to many of the neighbours and now my parents' house became like Piccadilly Circus as these neighbours trooped in to offer their congratulations. Mother was delighted and wanted to know all about Kathleen. Her questions were warm and gentle.

Today we are going to buy the engagement ring and I feel very excited. I have met Kathleen and we are now walking into town to catch a bus to Blackburn, where we have decided to buy the ring. I never thought that these things would happen to me. I feel so elated and more human than I have ever done. For the first time I just don't feel handicapped. Maybe this is what I have been waiting for; to be accepted by Kathleen has removed many of my insecurities. To realize that I am capable of such strong emotions and to realize that they are reciprocated is tremendous. I am just like any other man. I am going to be married. I ask Kathleen what sort of a ring she has in mind and I am quite surprised by her emphatic reply: 'Gold with three diamonds in it.'

We have found a reputable jeweller and are being ushered into a room at the back of the shop. When we state what we want, however, we are suddenly treated like royalty. Trays and trays of rings are being brought for us to see and although Kathleen tries on lots of rings, the first one that she likes is the one she chooses.

I would very much like to introduce Kathleen to Eileen. Eileen and I have grown apart since I moved into my flat and since she married Gordon. I am taking Kathleen to Eileen's house this afternoon for tea. Eileen is delighted. She and Kathleen got on very well and I have Eileen's blessings and congratulations on our engagement. This is important to me.

Kathleen's parents are doing all they can to help us prepare for the wedding. I do wonder, though, if they may be a little disappointed at Kathleen's choice of husband. I think

140

I can imagine how I would feel if my daughter wanted to marry a spastic. While Kathleen's parents are kind and welcoming to me and have never shown any hostility, I still wonder what they say when Kathleen and I are not around. I'm sure every mother wants her daughter to marry a handsome and normal young man.

We have been engaged for four months and Kathleen's brother is coming to look me over. I suspect that he was rather shocked when he met me but I cannot blame him. I doubt if I would want my sister to marry someone like me but I hope that as he gets to know me better his reservations will disappear.

One of Kathleen's friends, who is a nurse, has expressed concern to Kathleen about our marriage. She has warned Kathleen that she will be pushing me around in a wheelchair before long. I do not know why she should say this ... it is news to me. Fortunately Kathleen and I can openly discuss anything, so we do not have problems; if this piece of news bothers her, we will see the doctor to find out the truth.

Another so-called friend wants to know how I will manage the physical side of marriage and wonders if we will be able to have a family. There is no need to dwell on this subject. I am sure that I shall manage sex very well and my affliction cannot be inherited. Also because Kathleen and I have spoken very openly about our future together, she was able to answer our friend immediately. A nursing colleague of mine has advised me that after my marriage I should not have sex more than once a week as it might be too exhausting for me! It was hard not to laugh at her. She is well meaning, I am sure, but misinformed!

We have visited my doctor because I want Kathleen to be clear about the nature of my affliction and I wanted any questions she may have answered by a medical expert. Kathleen said after our visit that the doctor had told her nothing that I had not explained before.

Time has rolled by since our engagement and the wedding is only two months away. We are to be married on 4 June 1966. Four months ago I had my twenty-eighth birthday and

I did not think then that I would be married by the time I was twenty-nine. We are to have a Mormon wedding and have chosen Whitefield as the chapel. We will be the first couple to be married there as it is a new building. Actually, Kathleen worked on this building when it was being built. She even carted barrows of rubble and cement for the foundations and a lot of the brickwork inside the building; she cleaned bits of plaster with a wire brush. The members of the Mormon Church build their own chapels and Whitefield is nearing completion.

The flat is to be our home after our marriage and we are lucky to have all the furniture and basic requirements. But I am mindful of the fact that I chose everything in the flat and I wonder if it is to Kathleen's taste.

It is a busy time as we prepare for the big day. The most startling conversation which Kathleen and I have is one about her wedding dress. Kathleen and her mother are discussing where they are going to buy it, but I expect Kathleen to make her own. 'I'm sorry, Kathleen, but unless you are able to make your own dress there will be no wedding!'

'I don't understand. I've never made one in my life.'

'I am never going to earn big money and you will be able to save a lot if you can make your own clothes and those of any children we have.'

Kathleen looks a little dismayed and her mother looks shocked.

'Why don't you make an evening dress first,' I suggest, 'and see how you get on? Then you can decide about your wedding gown. But I would prefer it if you would make your own.' I feel strongly about the wedding dress because as a Mormon we are taught to be thrifty and to develop our talents. A good Mormon would never be so extravagant as to buy a wedding dress if she could make one.

The evening frock which Kathleen has made is greatly admired, and Kathleen is now looking forward to making her wedding dress. I still have friends in the textile trade and have managed to get a length of silk velvet for it.

I am still unhappy working at the hospital but there is no

way I can give up my job and become unemployed, because I need all the money I can get now.

It is a dull morning, not the type of day which I would have chosen for my wedding. I am being cosseted at my parents' home, having spent the night with them. The wedding is at ten o'clock and it seems an age away. I am so impatient this morning, having woken unusually early. I want it all to happen now. I find it disturbing having to wait with all these excited people around me. I have enough trouble coping with my own emotions without having to stay in the electric atmosphere at my parents'. I am sure it was not like this when my brothers were married.

I would like a few minutes on my own but there are so many people fussing around me. My breakfast has almost been injected and I had to eat it with mother and father, who are behaving as if it was my last meal.

'Come on, Alan, mother bought that bacon especially for you. Have some more. This is our last meal together.'

Mother is fretting. 'You won't forget the ring, will you? I wish the flowers would arrive. Alan, please eat a little more – you have a lot to go through today. I have cooked everything the way you like it.'

My parents are such dear people. What they don't realize is that I have eaten my fill. They are the ones who are not eating – the food which is left is theirs not mine.

Brother John has just arrived, I don't know why. He says it is just to make sure that I am all right.

There is a double-decker bus leaving Blackburn Boulevard to pick up guests en route to Whitefield and I use this as an excuse to escape from the house for a few minutes. 'Mother, I am just going on to Audley Range to make sure that the bus turns up for Aunty Elsie and Eileen.'

The little walk has made me feel a lot calmer. There are Aunty Elsie and Eileen waiting with their husbands for the bus. They are vexed when they see me for I am very casually dressed and they think there is something wrong. I assure them that all is well and that I have come out to get some air; I have plenty of time to get myself ready. While I wait

143

for the bus to arrive, I chat with Aunty and Eileen.

We are joined by John. 'I wondered where you were. I thought you had got cold feet and run off.' The bus arrives and I am able to see a few other guests. 'Isn't it time you were getting dressed, Alan? Are you sure you're all right? Mother says you have eaten very little breakfast.'

I have to laugh. 'John, I have had the most enormous breakfast. *They* are the ones who have not eaten. They are so excited, they don't know what they're doing.'

'Yes, they *are* in a bit of a tizzy but today is a big day for them ... well for us all really. We are so proud of you.'

I can see that Michael, who is best man, has arrived at the front door and John and I quicken our pace as we walk towards my parents' home. It has all been arranged. Michael was to arrive at ten past nine – is it now five past – he is to help me dress and we leave my mother's house at 9.30 to arrive at the church two minutes before Kathleen. I want to remain calm and Michael knows me so well that he is able to help me in lots of ways. If I have to sit in church and wait I will begin to feel uncomfortable; I cannot bear to be restrained and as I cannot talk or walk about in church, Michael and I have the timing worked out to the last detail.

We have arrived at the church on time and we pose for a few pictures. The photographer is a friend and he has been specially briefed about how to photograph me, because I sometimes look very deformed and monkey-like in photographs. It is time for us to take our seats in the church, only one minute later than we planned. The church is crowded. There are a great many more people here than we invited. Everyone is quiet and I feel very tense. Mother and father are sitting directly behind me. Kathleen is late! It is now nearly ten past ten. All my plans for keeping myself calm are foiled.

I can hear mother and father's conversation as they wait.

'I hope she's going to turn up.'

'Don't worry, mother, the traffic may be bad.'

'We got here all right.'

'She will come on a different road. Don't worry, she will be here. Do you want my handkerchief?'

144

'No, I don't. I'm not going to cry.'

'Well, I am. Lend me yours.'

'Don't be silly, father!'

'Just look at him, mother. Aren't you proud of him? He was more trouble to raise than the rest of them put together but we have had such happiness out of his achievements.'

'Shut up, you are being sentimental.'

'Maybe, but I never thought that he would marry. Not a normal girl, anyway. Did you? Look at him. He is a credit to us. It took me years to accept that I had a handicapped son but now I'm so proud of him.' My father is becoming very emotional.

I don't think I am meant to be hearing this conversation between my parents. Father has never been a demonstrative person and I truly did not think he had such affection for me. My chest is puffed out with pride and I shall treasure the memory of these words all my life.

The choir are all standing to sing the chosen hymn for Kathleen's walk down the church. But it is a mistake. Kathleen has not arrived, and after the first verse the choir sit down and Michael and I are asked to return to our seats.

Now I am full of jerks and uncontrollable movements and I did so want to avoid this. Which is why I did not want to arrive at the church any earlier than I needed to. Where is Kathleen?

Father leans over to whisper in my ear, 'Don't worry, Alan. If she does not turn up, you can always come back home to live.' I know my father is joking, he has always had a wicked sense of humour, but I can well do without that sort of comment at this moment.

The choir have risen again and this time before I take my place at the front of the church I glance back towards the door to make sure Kathleen is there. I cannot take my eyes from her as she walks down the church. My bride. Looking radiant and smiling at me through her veil. She takes my hand as she arrives at my side and squeezes it, which assures me that everything is all right. On my other side Michael is pressing my arm; he knows me so well that he senses that my

145

emotions are getting out of control. Michael's gesture helps to convey that message to me and as I turn to look at him his look tells me, 'You're doing all right.'

The ceremony now proceeds without a hitch and Kathleen and I are soon proclaimed man and wife. We sign the register and are now walking back down the church to the sound of the 'Wedding March'. I am oblivious to the crowd who are watching us. Kathleen and I have not spoken to each other but the looks which we exchange convey more than words ever can. Now we are in the foyer of the church building and are separated by the throng of people who want to congratulate us. I am an emotional person and feel I have done really well today in controlling myself, but seeing my sister's tearfully smiling face as she approaches me is too much. As we embrace each other she says, 'I have not seen you cry for years.'

I cannot reply because of the lump which is in my throat. I was all right until I saw my sister's tears; now I cling to her as I try to compose myself.

We are now outside having photographs taken and I feel wonderful, my wife by my side and Michael there too. The six bridesmaids and the pageboy are all being grouped together for photographs. Now my parents and Kathleen's parents are posed. There are so many friends and relatives crowding us and trying to take pictures. It is a relief when it is time for us to move on for the reception. Mormon churches have their own recreation halls within the church building.

Finally, the cake has been cut, the last speech has been made and we are now able to leave. Some friends are driving us to Surrey from where we have arranged to depart later, alone, for our honeymoon on the coast. Our final farewells are to our two mothers. We then leave amidst the traditional jangle of tin cans and pennies in the hub caps!

We have arranged to spend our wedding night in a country club in the heart of the Surrey countryside. We arrive in the area but are having difficulty in finding the place. We are directed by someone down a very narrow lane and there is the club, just a few yards along. We turn into a splendid-looking drive and pull up outside a large country house. Our friends are quite excited by the grandeur of the place and want to come in and have a look around. So the four of us go up to the big front door and pull on the bell. There is no reply, but the door is open so we go inside. There is a table in the middle of the hall with a small handbell on it, so we ring ... but still there is no reply. We can hear sounds coming from a closed room. The splendour of the inside of the place is even more impressive than the outside. We are all so intrigued that we separate to look into different rooms. Suddenly a man appears and we all return to the hall.

'Good evening, Mr and Mrs Counsell,' I say. 'We have a booking for the night.'

The man is looking at me in complete bewilderment. 'I'm sorry?'

Thinking that he cannot tell what I am saying or that maybe he is wondering what the devil has come to stay in his hotel, I repeat my original statement.

The man replies in a very cultured voice. 'Actually, I think not. This is a private house.'

Never before have I seen four people try to get through a door so quickly at the same time! We all feel so embarrassed. The situation is made worse by the fact that we were all having such a good nose around when the man appeared. But who would have expected a private house and a country club to have the same name and be down the same lane? We find the country club but I'm afraid that, pleasant though it is, it does not compare with the private place!

We begin our married life with a close bond, and this grows stronger as time passes. I have never been so happy in my life, and having someone with whom to share day-to-day living has made tremendous differences. No one has ever contributed to my confidence as my wife does; she encourages and supports me in every way and I find that I can do things now that I have never done in my life before. I think this is because I am far more relaxed generally than ever I was. I can see her blossoming too. She is a very talented person and I never cease to praise her dressmaking skills and her cooking. She fills our home with music as she plays the piano every day. She is far more relaxed than when I first knew her and more able to make friends, although she is still rather shy. Kathleen says that the atmosphere at home helps her to feel confident. This is a mutual thing. We are able to speak freely together and I find that any problem I may have is helped by talking it out with Kathleen.

We love our flat but we realize that this home cannot be permanent as we only have one bedroom, and no bathroom. We have often discussed having children and we have always thought we would do so eventually. Now that we have been married a little while, thoughts of having a family are more to the fore. But I am having qualms about the possibility. I wonder if having *me* for a father would be fair to a child because of the comments from other children, or even adults. I am tormented by thoughts of my own children being unhappy because of me, but I find it hard to put these feelings into words. Kathleen is a huge help to me at this time because she seems to have all the answers. She thinks that it will all depend on the relationship between me and the child. She and I together will make sure that there is a good and close relationship so that any hurt to the child will be minimal. Any children will be told exactly what is wrong with me when they are old enough to understand, so that they will be able to anticipate any comments that might be made. I can see that Kathleen wants a family very much.

Now, after careful debate and planning, we have decided to look around for a house to buy before we start our family. While we are house-hunting some people's attitude towards me is the same old combination of ignorance, fear and nervousness. In the estate agent's office we are inquiring about a house we like the look of, and up to now Kathleen has been asked an assortment of questions which should have been addressed to me or, at any rate, to both of us. I am standing right by the side of this man so why can't he ask me? Of course Kathleen allows me to answer the questions, but the man does not get the message. My wife is now being offered the key to the property so that we can look around it. As I put out my hand to receive it I am ignored and the key is passed to her. We now have to sign for the key and my wife is given the pen, which again she passes to me. The man looks

148

amazed as I sign the book and asks while I am writing, 'Can he manage?'

After a good hunt around we have finally decided on the house for us. It is not very big but will do for the time being. The house is an old stone-built terraced house in Rutland Street, Accrington. It was originally a two-up two-down, but there is an extension on the back which serves as the kitchen and the back bedroom has been divided into a bathroom and bedroom. It is a cosy little house; it needs decorating but we feel sure that through our combined efforts we can make it very nice.

Today we got the keys for our house and as I hurry home from work, I can't wait to get there and step over the threshold of our own home. I feel excited and am wondering how Kathleen is getting on. It was her day off today so she went to start cleaning up the place ready to move in next week. When I arrive, Kathleen is looking rather worse for wear but I can see that she is happy. We both feel proud to have our own home. The water is hot and I cannot resist that; the first thing I want to do in my own home is to have a bath! I have never lived in a house which has its own bathroom.

We have at last moved in with help from some friends. It is surprising how quickly we have filled up our home with all the necessary things. Kathleen's mother has given us some bits of furniture and now some friends who are emigrating are giving us quite a few more things. We soon have all that we need, although the house still needs decorating.

Kathleen has gone to answer the telephone but it is someone wanting to speak to me. I am not prepared for the shock: Eileen died this morning. I did not even know she had been so ill. She had a form of cancer around her ear which went deeper and deeper, and finally she died. She was only twenty-nine. Although Eileen and I have grown apart during the last few years I am hurt that no one has told me that she was sick; apparently, though, she has only been seriously ill for three weeks. But most of all, I am shocked and stunned and saddened. Eileen played an important part in my life, particularly in my teens and early twenties. I shall be forever

149

grateful for her friendship and the influence which she had on my life.

Kathleen's mother, too, has been ill for some time now and has been in and out of hospital. She is dying. Kathleen has never experienced the death of someone close, and I don't think that she has come to terms with the prospect. Once again her mother is in hospital and this time she is really bad; when the telephone rings very early in the morning Kathleen seems to know that it is serious news. When I return from answering the telephone she is in tears. For the first time in my life I must come to terms with someone else's grief and console her. Although this is a sad time for us, I feel good to know just how much my wife depends on me. She relies on me for comfort and I am able to help her through this dreadful period. I also find that her father and sister come to me for support and it boosts my morale a lot, selfishly perhaps, to find myself leaned upon rather than leaning.

Soon, however, we find that we have something to be optimistic about. We have just come out of the doctor's surgery and we are both thrilled. Our first child is on its way. The first thing we do is to jump on a bus and go and see my mother. She must be the first to know. She is delighted. So are most people; although we get some surprised reactions too. Maybe lots of people really did think that I wasn't capable of reproducing!

After the first excitement we settle down to plan for the baby. Kathleen gets busy with her knitting needles and I start thinking about getting the house decorated.

A friend of ours is supposed to come tonight to help decorate the front room, but he has not turned up. We have had such an upheaval to move all our furniture out of the room and taking up the carpet has caused havoc in our home. I am very tense thinking about alternatives should my friend not arrive to help. I am not expecting my wife to muck in as she is now five months pregnant. I am feeling very frustrated because I know that if I start to hang wallpaper it will tear in my clumsy hands and if I try and paint the woodwork there

150

will be brushmarks everywhere because I am so heavy-handed. I do so want our home to look nice.

Kathleen is getting rather impatient and suddenly blurts out, 'If I'd have known you were so useless, I would never have married you!'

I am shocked by this outburst, but instead of being hurt I become very angry and I shout back, 'I'll show you.'

I think Kathleen is a little frightened by my temper because she makes a hasty retreat. I know that in her home as a child her father did all the decorating, and she obviously looks on this chore as a man's job. Some time later she very cautiously peeps round the door and is amazed to see how much paper I have managed to get on the wall. Kathleen comes in and now she is patching up the tears and trimming the edges and we are soon working together to get the room finished. Kathleen tries her hand with the gloss paint and finds she enjoys doing it. Kathleen had thought in the first place that I wasn't really trying, and she was right. Because I hadn't done any decorating before, I took it for granted that I could not do it. I am glad that Kathleen said what she did, because now I have accomplished something new.

We have now decorated the whole house and are proud of our efforts. Our home looks so fresh and clean. Kathleen was forgiven a long time ago for asserting that I was useless, but I shall refer to it and use it to tease her for a long while to come!

I am still very unhappy with my work. Some of the other therapy assistants have been seconded by the hospital for a course which will qualify them as teachers of the mentally handicapped. I see this course as a way out of a tedious job. I have been working at this hospital for some years now and I ask my boss if I might be considered for secondment on to the college course. I am told that it would be a waste of time my applying as I would never be able to manage the work; anyway my attendance record at the hospital is not good enough. I explain that I find the work boring and maybe that is why I am so often ill. Again I am told that I would never manage a full-time course and that if I find the job boring I should find a new one. I tell my boss that I have already been to college twice before, but he insists that I would not manage and that the hospital will not even recommend me. I try to put my name forward by writing to the hospital medical superintendent but I am referred back to my boss, who deals with all applications for secondments, so I am stumped again.

My mind dwells continually on our expected baby and I start to have doubts which mar my happiness. Supposing my child should be born handicapped like some of the children I work with at the hospital? I myself am handicapped and I see hundreds of handicapped children each day. I become obsessed with the fear that my child will be born having something wrong with it. I cannot share my worries with Kathleen as I do not want her to be disturbed. I cannot rid myself of this awful depression. I had dismissed thoughts like this before my wife became pregnant, otherwise we would never be having this baby. Even some of our friends have asked me if there is a danger that the baby will be handicapped in any way. These questions do nothing to reassure me; I tell them that the baby will be all right with a lot more confidence than I really feel.

We have had terrific support from our families throughout the pregnancy and now all is ready as the day draws near. My father treats Kathleen like royalty when we visit and Aunty Elsie is so excited about the whole thing anyone would think she was having the baby!

The day the baby is due arrives, but nothing happens. The doctor is sure that the baby is ready to be born but the baby obviously has other ideas. The days drag on and I try to humour Kathleen. I know that she finds this time even more frustrating than I do; at least I have my work to go to whilst Kathleen just sits around the house all day waiting for something to happen.

Ten days late and I receive a call at work from Kathleen. She has just returned from the doctor's and he wants her to go into hospital because her blood pressure is high. I rush straight home so as to be with her when the ambulance arrives. We arrive at the hospital and Kathleen is whisked off to have her labour induced. I feel useless. I want to be with

Kathleen but a nurse is telling me that I must go – I can return at visiting time at seven o'clock. It is now only two. I go to my mother's house to give her the news but I find it very difficult to do anything that will help pass the hours. At seven o'clock prompt I rush into the ward to see Kathleen. She obviously has not had a very pleasant time but she is trying to be cheerful. Her labour began at about four o'clock and things are now getting rather uncomfortable for her. Before I leave the hospital I make inquiries and am informed that the baby will most likely be born during the night; I may ring up first thing in the morning. I cannot see Kathleen again until the next evening.

I return home but sleep evades me. I wait the night through wondering how my wife is getting on and feeling utterly useless and remote from her. It had been arranged for my wife to go into a nursing home near to my work so as to make visiting easier. Now she is in hospital in another town and I am wondering if they are expecting complications. I do not fully understand why she has been taken into hospital and why labour has had to be induced, and now all the doubts and frustrations I have felt during the pregnancy come flooding back. I have spent a sleepless, tormented night. I have no idea what my wife might be suffering or if our baby has been born yet. I think it is inhuman to separate a man and his wife at a time like this.

Looking at the clock for the hundredth time since I went to bed I decide to get up. It is too early to telephone the hospital, as it is only five o'clock. I must do something. I clean the house from top to bottom and everything shines. It is now seven o'clock. Dare I ring up yet?

I have a son. Seven hours old. The nurse said that he is all right and that mother and baby are doing fine. It was a relatively easy birth. It has been over for hours – the agony of the night was unnecessary. I have a son. Words cannot express my feelings. I did not think it was possible for one person to feel such elation, such relief, such pride and joy. I want everyone to know. I have a son; the nurse said that there is absolutely nothing wrong with him, he is a perfect baby. It is going to be very difficult to have to wait until this

153

evening to see him. Kathleen and the baby are to be transferred to the nursing home sometime during the day as all is now well and her blood pressure is down again.

Today has been the longest day of my life. I have been so impatient all day wondering what my son looks like and longing to see Kathleen. The hands on the clock have never moved so slowly.

Now I have to queue outside the nursing home waiting for the doors to open. This is ridiculous. How could they make me wait like this? The desire to see them both hurts inside. When will they open the doors? It is past the advertised visiting time. At last I am allowed in and shown to my wife's bedside.

'Where is he, then?'

'He is in the nursery.'

'Don't I get to see him, then?'

'Yes. Go to the nursery and they will show him to you.'

I leave my wife and go in search of my own son in the nursery only to find that he is shown to me through a window. I want to hold him. How frustrating this is. My wife is right – I did come to see my son tonight. I did not really come to see her, and while Kathleen is laughing and teasing me I know that she understands the way I feel and my disappointment in having to wait seven days before I can hold my own son . . . seven days before my wife and child come home, and until that time I will only be allowed to view him through a glass window.

It is difficult to describe what my son looks like, as I do not see him for very long through the window of the nursery. He seems to have gingery hair and blue eyes, but no more details are discernable as he is always wrapped in a bundle. He is to be named Grant Alan.

What jubilation. The day has arrived when my wife and Grant are to come home from the nursing home. I have been up since dawn making sure that the house is immaculate for their homecoming. I have also made a 'welcome home' cake for them. A friend is coming in his car to go with me to bring them back. We have to be there by nine o'clock.

Now I am completely happy as I sit by my own fireside with

154

my little son on my knee. I never thought that I would be a father. There has never, of course, been a baby like this one since time began. He is so peaceful and content. I could sit here and let him sleep on my lap all day. His little hands and feet fascinate me.

Kathleen and I have given the baby our whole time today, it being his first day home. I prepared our meals before going to the nursing home this morning so there is nothing to do but be together as a family. Our general practitioner called early in the afternoon, just for a few minutes, to make sure that all is well. Now at 4.30 we have other visitors at our door. It is my mother and father, who have come to see the baby. Kathleen and I cannot get near our son. Mother and father have completely taken him over.

Naturally my parents are staying for their evening meal. Father does not seem at all well to me but he says that he is all right. Halfway through our meal I can tell father is in real pain. Mother wants me to telephone for a taxi to take him home quickly. It looks as though father is going to have another heart attack.

I am supposed to return to work this morning after one week's leave to look after my wife. I get up to prepare for work and feel very sick. While I am in the bathroom I vomit violently and feel too sick to go to work.

After six weeks of this odd sickness I am beginning to feel really concerned. If I get up in the morning knowing that I do not have to go to work then I feel fine, but each morning I decide to go back to work I am violently sick. I have forced myself to go in twice after vomiting in the bathroom, but each time I have almost collapsed at the gates of the hospital and have had to be sent home.

It has been decided that my illness is psychological. I was so tense throughout my wife's pregnancy thinking that she would give birth to a handicapped child that I have now put up a mental barrier between myself and the hospital. I have had such an emotional time working at the hospital that I am now physically sick each time I have to go there. The family doctor advises me that I should leave the hospital service and find some other employment. That is easier said than done.

However, after much discussion with Kathleen I have decided to resign from my job and look around for another one. It is silly to carry on like I am and I may make myself really ill if I do not make a positive decision.

My wife feels that I should apply for a place on the course for teachers of the mentally handicapped because she feels that I have something to offer in that field. I could maybe get a county grant to finance us whilst on the course. But at the moment I do not think I could cope with the pressures of applying.

It is obvious that there has been a lot of speculation by many people about the birth of our first baby. So many people exclaim about his 'normality' when they see him. People have even said to Kathleen, 'You would never think that Alan could have such a child.' One woman from Blackpool threw up her arms at the sight of Grant and announced, 'Oh look, it is a miracle!'

Grant is adored by his grandfather, who has been in bed ever since the day he was taken ill at our home. Each time we enter my parents' home we are greeted by the sound of my father's voice from his bed in the parlour. 'Where is that baby? Come on, bring him here. Let me have him.'

Father seems to be in his element if he can gaze at Grant. Mary, my brother's wife, was with father today when we arrived. As soon as Grant was given to him, father inspected Grant's arms and legs and declared to Mary, 'Look at this child, Mary. There is nothing wrong with him. Look at him. He is a perfect little fellow.'

My father died this afternoon. The day after his inspection of Grant and his declaration to Mary. I have the most eerie feeling that my father clung to his life because he wanted to see for himself that my first child really was normal. He had carried fear with him for some time . . . he was subconsciously afraid that what I had might be passed on to my children.

8

I am seeing my father cremated. The place is packed with people of all kinds and the banks of flowers add a strange and splendid splash of colour to the sad affair. This is the end of my father's life, but it is the end of other things as well. Like all people who lose a parent, I suppose, I feel unprotected in an odd way, closer to my own death, in the front line now that my father is gone. I feel completely bewildered. When my father is turned to ashes, so will part of my foundations crumble. A whole past world will go with him. Without him, my future will be changed. How can I live the rest of my life without one of the main characters of my world? How can I forget the dependency of my early life, the many times when father carried me down the stairs of our home? How can I forget the many other memories which we shared and which we could resurrect by a mere look passed to each other? No. It is not just father being cremated, but part of me as well.

How cruel life seems when we have to be parted from those we need, from those who have been the mainstay of our lives. To be separated so abruptly without a chance of saying goodbye, without the opportunity to express thanks for their part in our lives. I need my father here with me ... how am I to live without his splendid advice and encouragement?

His coffin has been carried into church by my brothers and brother-in-law, in accordance with mother's wishes. I know that she is upset because I refuse to be part of this ceremony, but I cannot bear the thought of carrying my father to be burned. I told the family that I could not do it because of a lack of strength and everyone has accepted this, thinking

I meant physical strength. But they are mistaken; it is emotional strength that I need.

They say that time is a great healer but always will the wound of my father's death be with me. I shall learn to live with it rather like the people who learn to live with the pain of a constant backache. I know my experience is not unique, I know that most people react similarly when they lose a parent, but I do believe that my father's strength and love helped me to an exceptional degree.

Life, despite my father's death, is pleasant although I am unemployed and we have trouble managing on unemployment benefit. The time I spend with my wife and son enriches all my days. Never before have I felt so needed and so wanted. My son is lovely to be with and I never cease to thrill at the touch of his little hands. He is now spoonfed; I had always imagined that I would not be able to feed him at this stage because of my shaky hands, but Grant has a mind of his own and has discovered that by grabbing hold of my wrist he can steady my hand enough to allow me to feed him. This is a little thing, but being involved with Grant is genuinely thrilling, and discovering ways around various problems is continually stimulating. I am constantly told by people how well I look and how I have changed physically. I recognize this. It is that I am much more relaxed; I am less competitive and much more satisfied with my life. I have never had such a friend as Kathleen. It is difficult to understand or express, but Kathleen is such an influence in my life that I feel a new person. The confidence and loyalty that my marriage inspires are what I have needed all of my life, despite my family's love. With this assurance and with the security of our relationship, I feel a great deal less handicapped. The future seems rosy. I feel I could overcome any problem as long as my wife is by my side. Encouraged by Kathleen I have applied for a course which will lead to the Diploma of the Training Council for Teachers of Mentally Handicapped Adults. This is the course which my hospital boss said I would never manage.

I am here at the Harris College in Preston and as always

when I attend for interview, my confidence wanes when I see the other applicants. They all look capable and I feel at a disadvantage competing with such people. Why should I feel inferior? I have good experience in the field of mental health. I also need to think of my wife and son; my getting a place on this course will affect their future as well as my own. I feel aggressive as I am being interviewed. I must sell myself for the sake of my son. I feel positively big-headed as I tell the panel of interviewers how able I am, but I am determined to do all in my power to gain a place.

One of the men on the panel is asking me, 'Mr Counsell, we have fifty applicants for eighteen places. Can you tell me why we should offer *you* a place in preference to a normal person?'

Normally such a question would send me into my shell and I would become tongue-tied, but not today. 'Sir, are you suggesting that I am not normal? I was born like this, I do not know what it is like to be any different. It is normal for me to be like this. If I were like you I would not seem normal to myself. I would also like to suggest that if you or the majority of the so-called normal applicants had my handicap they might like to contract out of the human race and become a recluse. I think my past experience will tell you why I should have a place on the course and why my handicap should be disregarded.'

The man makes no comment but looks at me without any recognizable emotion showing on his face. He continues to ask questions. 'How do you think pupils and clients are going to react to your impeded speech?'

'Sir, while I was waiting for my interview I spoke to two foreign applicants who are now living in this country and their accents make their English very hard to understand. I hope you will ask them the same question. Again I ask you to look at my past experience and references and consider that if my speech was a hindrance to the patients whom I dealt with in the hospital I would not have such references. Nor would I have made such progress in the hospital service.'

I am afraid that I have answered all the questions too cheekily and aggressively and I have spoiled my chances of a

159

place on the course. I am asked to sit in the waiting room. I have only been here a couple of minutes and I am being called back; I am being offered a place on the course. I am so shocked that I respond in a very cold manner.

Things are falling into place quite well for I have been given a grant by the county council while I am at college. My course begins in September 1969 and although we are going to be short of money, I am looking forward to my course and hope it will improve my employment prospects.

I have been asked to lead the music at the Sunday services at the Blackburn branch of the Church, which is a laugh because I do not sing very well. Kathleen plays the organ at these services so I can practise at home with her. It is just a question of standing before the congregation and keeping them in time. One uses one's hands more than one's voice and under Kathleen's tuition I cope.

It is rewarding for me to lead the music as it is something I thought I would never be able to do. By now, perhaps, I should have learned that one can be surprised at one's capabilities if one is steered toward new experiences.

I learned today that two people who I worked with at the hospital were offered paid secondment to do the same course as me but they have been unsuccessful in gaining a place. This seems ironic.

While I wait for September to come around I do voluntary work on a few assessment courses for the Spastics Society. There is also time to be with my family and to visit my mother, who needs her family around her more than ever now that father is gone.

After the initial problems of getting to know people and of them getting used to me, I find college life very stimulating. I particularly enjoy studying educational psychology. Philosophy is a subject new to me but nevertheless enjoyable. For sociology classes we have a young man who seems a bit radical, and he makes us think deeply about the subject. Our music lecturer began his course by putting us in a soundproof box so that we could learn to appreciate silence. It was awful and not one of the students could stand the

160

noiselessness for more than a few minutes. We became aware of our heartbeats, and it was terrifying.

Looking at the course curriculum it seems that the year will be hectic. We have a very impressive list of subjects to study as well as essays, a thesis and several teaching practices to do.

I have taught myself to type so that I can cope with the written work. I type in an unconventional way, using a stick which I hold in two hands, like I did the pencil when I first began to write, and I bash the keys of the typewriter with the end of it. My speed is very slow; it takes me about forty minutes to type a foolscap sheet but that is quicker than I can write. It is also difficult to concentrate both on the physical control I need for typing and on spelling and language structure, which I find difficult anyway.

There are other, more fundamental strains imposed by full-time academic learning. My early years of not being able to verbalize have affected my ability to use language formally and I am also finding more and more that my spelling is influenced by my mispronounciation of words, caused by non-correction when I was younger. I suppose it was difficult for adults around me to discern mistakes when I began to speak since everything came out sounding so odd anyway. They were so delighted to hear me speaking that they thought it might do harm to correct me. Now I am becoming aware that I pronounce many words wrongly and wonder if people might think it is because of my impediment. It isn't, though. For example I am aware that I say 'cuggle' instead of 'cuddle' and I have never been corrected. But now that I am aware of it, I can say 'cuddle' quite well.

In our physical education sessions at college I am allowed to join in what I think I can manage and if I think that an activity is beyond my abilities I just sit and watch. I have never participated in sports because I am not good at them but now I enjoy having a go. I play badminton with my fellow students. I found it difficult to hit the shuttlecock at first and it took a lot of concentration to develop the necessary co-ordination, but I was aggressively determined to play. I also had difficulty in serving, but now I am able to pick up the shuttlecock by the feathers using the tips of my fingers and the root of my right palm, and by a flick of the wrist I am able to send it into the air. I would like to have a go on the trampoline but I am much too scared to try.

There is a lot of practical content to the course and the students have to spend time working in different establishments which employ teachers of the mentally handicapped.

Another student and I have been sent to work in a subnormality hospital in Yorkshire. We have to live in the hospital hostel. We are to involve ourselves in the education of adult patients and as the hospital does not have any educational provision for these, much interest is shown in our work. The patients whom we work with are drawn from the hospital workshops and the officer in charge has difficulty in accepting me. My colleague thinks it is funny, but I feel annoyed. The man treats me as though I was a patient from another hospital in the charge of my colleague. If I go on my own to collect a group of patients from the workshops I am not allowed to take them to the room which has been assigned as our classroom. I have always to wait until my colleague arrives as he is the 'responsible person'. The man in charge of the workshops is consistently rude to me. I have tried to engage him in conversation hoping to prove my intellect, but each time I speak to him he pats me on the head and sends me on my way.

I want to change his attitude and ask if I might discuss my group of patients with him. I hope that this will help him to accept me but he will not talk to me. It is as if he does not want to know me.

Because of all this it has been decided that my group of students will come from the occupational therapy department. The occupational therapist is very helpful and I am more able to work with her. She also tells me why the man from the workshops is so rude to me. He applied for a place on the course at the same time as I but was turned down; he has commented that he cannot help feeling bitter when he sees that a person like me was successful and he was not.

It is possible for my colleague and me to use a trampoline

162

at the hospital and during evenings I am finally able to get my colleague to help me to overcome my fear of it. I look forward to returning to college to show off my new skill to my fellow students.

My mother is a bit devious in suggesting that I do my regulation three weeks' teaching practice at the normal school where I went as a young child. This is quite near her house and I think she hopes that I can have lunch with her each day while I am there. I must admit to being apprehensive of having to teach normal children. I am not sure how they are going to react to my voice and I do not want to fail in any part of my course. I will be assessed during teaching practice on any problems in discipline or communication.

The head of the school has welcomed me into his study and is now sending for the deputy head, who supervises all student teachers who come into the school. My first teacher, the kind woman who taught me in my first class, is still at the school and has entered the room. She is being introduced to me as the deputy head. I can see that she does not recognize me and is shocked when I am familiar in my approach to her.

'Miss Groom, you have hurt my feelings. You have forgotten me. You do not recognize me.'

'I beg your pardon. I am sure that I have not met you before.'

'Oh yes, you have, Miss Groom. My name is Alan Counsell.'

'Counsell . . . Counsell. Yes, I remember the family. John, Joe and Tom. I think we even have some of *their* children in the school now. I think there was one more but he was a bad cripple.' She is pensive.

I interrupt her speech excitedly. 'Yes, that is me.'

She looks completely dumbfounded. 'We had to carry him around. He could not walk.'

'Yes, that was me.'

'This is incredible. Are you telling me that you are the little boy who I carried around for years?'

'Yes, that is me. I used to have a big teddy as well.'

'Yes, that's right. Alan Counsell, well, I just cannot

163

believe my eyes.' The woman is so surprised that the headmaster has been forgotten and she is taking me by the hand with excited gasps of delight, just like she would a five-year-old, and marching me out of the room. 'I know someone else who will be as delighted as I am to see you.'

I am being led down a corridor to a classroom where I recognize the last teacher that I had in junior school. There is a lesson in progress but the deputy head walks into the room and interrupts excitedly. 'Do you know who this is?' she asks the mystified teacher.

'No. Should I?' replies the teacher.

'This is my little Alan. Alan Counsell. Do you remember him?'

'Alan Counsell. Oh, yes, Ian's uncle. Ian said that his uncle was coming here today.' I can see that the teacher is still mystified by the deputy head's excited entrance.

'You do not understand, do you? This is the little boy who I used to carry around. Alan Counsell. Do you remember little Alan?'

'I am beginning to realize. You mean this is the Counsell boy who could not walk?'

People are still talking about me as if I wasn't there! It doesn't make it any less annoying, that they are kind and friendly.

'Yes, yes. This is Alan.'

The three of us are standing in front of the class, which includes my nephew Ian. We reminisce about my time in school. Both these teachers seem delighted to see me. I try to explain about my fears of teaching normal children but these worries appear irrelevant to both of them, who promise to help me all they can while I am on teaching practice.

One of the first activities on my first morning in school is the school assembly, which is taken by the deputy head. I have been asked to stand at the back of the hall behind the older children. After the usual preliminaries the deputy head starts to speak. 'Boys and girls. I am going to tell you a true story this morning and I want you all to listen carefully. Once upon a time we had a small boy who came to our school and

164

he was not able to talk and he could not walk. We had to carry him around. . . . '

To my embarrassment the deputy head is telling the children about my early school life. My nephew keeps turning around grinning at me. I could kill him! She concludes, 'Now, children, if this boy, who is now a man, were to come back to our school as a teacher would you be kind to him?'

There is a loud chorus of 'Yes, miss.'

'But he still speaks a bit funny. Would you listen carefully to what he said to you?'

The chorus is repeated. 'Yes, miss.'

'Would you like to meet this man now?'

'Yes, miss.'

'Mr Counsell, would you like to come to the front and tell us why you are here?'

I walk to the front of the hall, which now contains an absolutely silent group of children, and somehow I explain why I am here. But the whole episode is so hideously embarrassing that I soon make a hasty exit.

Naturally the story has had an impact on most of the children and obviously some of them have gone home and told their parents about their new teacher. The second morning while I am marking the register the Scott twins ask, 'Please, sir, are you our Uncle Alan?'

The Scott twins are seven years old and I am amazed at their question. 'I am sorry, I do not understand.'

'We went home last night and told our dad about you and he said that we knew you and that you had bought our christening shawls when we were born and that you were our uncle.'

'What is your father's first name?'

'My dad is called Dennis and my mum is called Pearl.' I now know who they are as I used to go dancing with Pearl and Dennis and we were very good friends. These are not the only children whose parents know me and I am inundated by invitations to tea from old chums who have heard about my return.

Today is the day of my assessment and my tutor has come

165

to visit me with two external examiners. I am giving a history lesson with these three watching me and making notes at the back of the classroom. Naturally I feel nervous, but my tutor makes me feel worse by saying to me as he leaves the room to have coffee with the deputy head, 'I have never seen anything like it. I will see you later.'

I am on playground duty so I have quite a time to worry about what mistakes I could have made in teaching my history lesson. At the end of playtime I am confronted by my tutor, who has come to discuss my assessment with me. I am the last student from the group to be assessed and to my relief I am presented with a report that is very complimentary. He adds, 'I do not know how you did it, but that is the best lesson which I have observed in a long time. The relationship which you have with those children is remarkable.'

I feel a bit of a fraud, since this man doesn't realize how sympathetic my pre-publicity to the children was!

Because of my slow writing there is concern about my Christmas examinations. My tutor thinks that it will be easier to have someone to write for me rather than to assess how much extra time I would need to finish my paper in my own handwriting. Students from other courses have volunteered to write for me and at the examinations I have a different person every half-hour. I appreciate all the help which I am being given, but the problem is that I have never spoken to some of these people and it takes them time to tune into my speech, so I have to keep repeating the words that I want them to write. Apparently, though, my tutors are pleased with the results of my exams but I really do not want to repeat the experience.

In retrospect I feel that I have broken down quite a few barriers in my first term at college; I can remember the whisperings behind my back during the first few weeks and the awkward silences whenever I joined in a group conversation. Now people accept me quite naturally and are even prepared to help me.

Everyone in college is looking for a job as the course nears completion. I have applied for a teaching post with the

Spastics Society at Meldreth Manor School, which is a residential school for spastic children who are also mentally handicapped. It is situated in a village between Royston and Cambridge. The post is residential and if I am lucky enough to be appointed, my wife and I will have a house in the school grounds. For this reason Kathleen has been asked to travel with me to see what may be our future home.

Neither Kathleen nor I expected to find a place like this. The main administrative building is of an attractive Scandinavian design. The house which we are being shown looks ultra-modern compared with our present home and has a big garden. We are very impressed by what we see and are quite excited at the possibility of moving here.

How lucky can I be? I have been offered the post, but it depends on me passing my final examinations in July.

I do not want to take the intermediate examination by proxy as I did the last one. There is much discussion about the problem and finally my tutor suggests that my wife might be asked to write for me. This is most acceptable as she is familiar with my speech and I like the idea that she will be sharing a significant event in my life. There will of course be a scrutineer present throughout the examinations. When I eventually find out that I have passed, my wife teases me by saying that she helped me!

There is sadness and nostalgia as we prepare to leave Lancashire and move south but there is optimism too, for we are looking forward to making new friends and a new way of life. What excitement we feel as we settle into our new home. The house has pine ceilings and a pine staircase, rather grand when compared with our former little terraced house. We are looking forward to growing our own vegetables too.

The school is built in an orchard and many of the fruit trees still remain, scattered around the buildings. We are not used to such space and are fascinated by it.

Meldreth village is long and narrow with thatched cottages dotted amongst the more modern houses. There are two shops and a post office on the high street, and the village pub. Life here is very different to what we had in Lancashire but

167

we enjoy the country and walk each day, never tiring of the changing hedgerows and flowers.

There are four schoolhouses which each cater for thirty children. Each house has three or four teachers and a physiotherapist. The school also has nurses, speech therapists and childcare staff. There are two other teachers working in the house that I have been assigned to. One of these teachers has been at the school ever since it opened and is able to give me lots of valuable help.

I have a class of nine fourteen-year-olds who have handicaps additional to their physical and mental difficulties. Four of them are in wheelchairs, two are blind, four have emotional problems and three have severe speech and language defects. I find it most interesting to work with a speech therapist with these three children for I learn much that is of benefit to me too. The aim with children is to get them to swallow, suck and chew correctly. This is an important stage in learning to speak. As a baby develops, this is what happens: he or she is born with a sucking reflex and a chewing pattern gradually develops. Until this has taken place, a young child will not speak. In my own life this lack of development had farreaching consequences. I realize that I could have derived benefit from speech therapists when young and even now, at the age of thirty-three, I am learning much from working with these children that helps my own physical coordination and gives more clarity to my speech.

The academic achievements of the children in my class are low, but I cannot expect them to attain much as their average mental age is around the three-year-old level. I am specially interested in communication and awareness and do not see why all of the children in my class should not be able to anticipate their needs and ask for them.

I am also able to compare my family with the families of the children I teach. Working with these children and seeing their difficulties is making me aware and more appreciative of my parents' support in raising me. It would have been so easy for them to have sent me away from home. I have never before realized how difficult and demanding it must have been for them to have a child like me. How I appreciate my home life, however unsophisticated it was, and my brothers and sister. My childhood was happy and I would have hated to have been sent to a boarding school. How I wish that some of the children here could be cared for and supported by a family like that. Of course some of the children here have super parents, but others lack family support and involvement. I realize that some of the children here could not live with their parents because of the severity of their handicap and other domestic problems, but there are some who could benefit from a natural home life.

The first meeting with many of the parents of the children I teach is strained. I know that many are very surprised to find a spastic teaching their child. Ultimately I am able to form a good relationship with all of them, except one mother who asked to see my qualifications. I proudly produced them, all three, but she still finds it difficult to accept me.

Many of the parents are interested in my childhood and in the progress I have made. I have to be very careful that I do not give them false hopes; they could easily think that their child is going to develop as I have. That is not the case because all of these children have a mental handicap as well as a physical one. I am not saying that the children will not make progress – they will – but this work is teaching me to use tact as nothing else ever did.

The school's annual fête is held only two weeks after the September term has begun and is the main fundraising event of the year. Here I meet a great many more parents, some of whom I am meeting socially for the first time. They are also able to meet my wife and son, and I am aware of some parents' surprise. As usual, I suspect, they did not expect that I'd have a normal marriage and family. I am always conscious when making observations such as this that I might be oversensitive and imagining things, but Kathleen too is aware of the speculation about my family.

Teaching the children is difficult and requires great patience. I am not at all sure that I am teaching the right things; I am aware that the children are going to be adult one day and that they need to try and live in normal society. I am aware too of all the many lessons which I learned just from being with normal children and from living in a normal

169

household. Meldreth is isolated as a school and the children hardly ever see normal children, let alone mix with them. They need to develop integration skills and in my opinion these cannot be taught in a classroom or in the institutionalized atmosphere of a boarding school for handicapped children, however enlightened. Even the physiotherapy could be a lot more exciting. When I think of the physio I received as my brothers dragged me over fences and hedges and as they pulled me up hills and over rough ground, I realize that they were actually doing the same for me as the physios are doing for these children, although obviously the treatment here is structured and professional. I am often criticized for expressing such views but no one has yet convinced me that I am wrong. I would like to specialize in my own type of social education, which would be based on my theories, formed as they are from academic study and from my experience of life. But a damper is initially put on my enthusiasm by many members of staff so I am stuck in my classroom trying to do my best within the existing set of methods at the school.

Our second child is now on its way and this time I feel a great deal calmer about the pregnancy. My son has been no problem and I have ceased to worry that my children will be born abnormal. However, Kathleen seems to have her own fears with this pregnancy; she's having a hard time as she feels that something is going wrong. The doctor reassures her as he thinks that Kathleen's fears are connected with the fact that we are living close to so many handicapped children and so she is more aware that many babies are born abnormally. She eventually overcomes her fears and we decide on a home delivery because the maternity hospital is twelve miles away.

We have engaged a midwife and I am to be present at the birth. Our midwife is a treasure. She has had three children of her own and often talks about the times when she had her babies. During the pregnancy she has become a family friend.

Kathleen goes into labour. It goes on for hours and the midwife is getting anxious because she feels that the baby

170

should be here by now. She asks me to go and get the doctor. But when I return to my wife's side the panic is over and the baby is just being born. It would seem that my daughter was waiting for me to be out of the way to make her entrance. I am no expert but I think that the baby is bluer than she should be. The midwife agrees and gets her oxygen supply to give the child. The cylinder is empty! I remember how an oxygen deficiency may have affected me. Luckily the baby is all right and when the doctor arrives, his examination of the baby reveals that Marcia Lianne is perfectly normal. I wait until I am alone with the midwife and away from my wife before letting go my aggression, which has boiled since the oxygen incident. I tell our midwife just what lack of oxygen can do to a baby and I do not mince my words. A practical example of what I am saying is passing the window of our home and I reinforce my point by attracting the attention of the midwife to the unfortunate child riding his tricycle.

Having our daughter at home is lovely. There are no hospital regulations and no visiting times to adhere to. I have been involved with the baby right from the start and I feel more part of things than I did at the birth of Grant. Grant too is delighted with his baby sister. He is fascinated by her tiny fingers and toes and is able to see her have her first bath. Grant is nearly three now and we thought that he might be jealous of the new arrival. But the fact that the baby brought a present with her for him has helped to overcome any problem there might have been! All our family and friends are warned not to leave Grant out when they come to see the baby.

I feel a double thrill when I have my new daughter on my lap and my son by my side. Almost all of my colleagues have been to see the baby and our home is like a flower show because of all their gifts. There is one adverse comment though; someone says that a person such as I should not have children and do I not realize that my children will never speak properly because they will copy my impediment? I can safely ignore this remark because Grant is already speaking very clearly. Naturally Grant is with his mum most of the time, true, but he has *never* imitated my voice; even when I repeat to him some word which he mispronounces he is always able to understand me. It is interesting to note than Grant's accent is not Lancashire but Cambridgeshire, which suggests that he has been more influenced in his speech by his friends and people in the locality than by his parents.

After working at the school for almost two years I have decided to look for another job. I find my situation at Meldreth increasingly frustrating because I cannot put my theories into practice. It is not going to be easy to find a new job and, besides, my wife and I love our life and home at Meldreth. But I am unhappy at work.

I have applied for many posts but have not been successful. My mother has often talked about her belief in fate and though I am not sure that I go along with all that she says, certainly the events of the past few months have changed my plans.

First of all the principal of the school is leaving. The newly appointed principal is such a personality and so impressed me when I met him that I have decided to stay at Meldreth for a while longer. It is good to know that the new principal shares some of my views about social education.

We also have a new deputy principal and he becomes my house supervisor. The personality and manner of this man are such that everyone responds to his charm. He is warm and outgoing and one cannot help being happy working with him.

My ideas and philosophies are more valued by the new management team and I am allowed to pursue the type of teaching which I really feel is right for 'my' children. I want them to experience more normal living and I enlist the help of some of the people who live in the village to take our children into their homes and allow them to socialize. My wife is enthusiastic and she also helps with the project. Soon we are able to structure these visits and teach specific assignments. There are opportunities too for correcting anti-social behaviour and the results we see are encouraging.

Norman, for example, has a paralysis of the lips and front of the tongue and palate, a terrible handicap because he cannot feel food in his mouth. He has an awful habit of pushing his food to the back of his mouth with his fingers where he can feel it. His shirt front is always a mess at mealtimes. He has had surgery to help his dribbling, so that is not a real problem, and through going out to coffee in the home of a lady who lives in the village Norman has been helped to overcome his self-consciousness to a large extent. It is just that he likes going out to see his new friend but has been told that if he does not improve his habits he will not be able to go. It is stimulating for Norman to receive genuine praise for his efforts and when he is invited to a meal at the home of his friend I can almost see his chest swell with pride. On his birthday his friend and her husband took Norman out to his first meal in public. Norman came back to school looking as clean as when he left. The evening had been a success and Norman's self-image had improved. He takes time and care over his meals now and one can take him anywhere and not be embarrassed by his eating habits. Norman cannot speak but his eyes and his posture indicate that he is proud of his achievements.

Victor is a boy who has no contact with his parents and has never been in a normal home. He spends his holiday periods in a large children's home so he is very institutionalized. He was introduced to a family in the village where he was encouraged to participate in domestic activities. The lady of the house was smashing with Victor and allowed him to help her as she would a normal three-year-old. Very soon Victor was telling the woman all kinds of things which he had never mentioned before but which obviously bothered him. He suddenly stopped wetting the bed each night, although he had done this for all of his fourteen years. Suddenly he began to identify colours in his friend's home, although previously he had not developed any colour concept. Along with these improvements came a sense of pride, and Victor went on to achieve more than his teachers ever thought possible. As he made relationships, so his confidence increased and his personality developed. Victor is mildly spastic with a severe mental handicap and hyperactive tendencies.

These are just two of the many success stories to which the people of Meldreth village contributed.

I often take some of the children back to my house to entertain them or to give them a meal, and it is good to see the progress they make in an ordinary home. Kathleen is really good with these children, although she was very apprehensive at first. My own children accept the school children quite readily and some of them are always included in my children's party invitations.

After a time I am getting the school children to join in more community activities. I have made friends in the village. The principal is an energetic man and the school has developed under his leadership. The children are now much better behaved when they are away from school because of the training they are receiving in social education.

I have become more and more involved in camping and school expeditions. My educational programmes are orientated towards independence. How can I justify teaching maths or English to a fourteen-year-old mentally handicapped person when he is unable to set a table for four people or ask for his most fundamental needs? I would suggest that setting a table is in some way intellectually related to the beginning of a maths sense, in that a sense of order and neatness and numbers is required, and that for such a person to know his needs and communicate them is useful English education.

Full use of the school caravan is made to facilitate my methods. I find that I can teach more effectively outside my classroom than in it. I do not confine my teaching to the daytime either, as I find that the skills acquired in making their own evening meal in the school caravan are essential to our children. The opportunity for correction and meaningful teaching are also greater in a living situation than in the school.

The enthusiasm I have for social education on school expeditions is infecting other members of staff as well, and I have been asked by a colleague if I will help him to organize a week's trip in narrow boats on the Grand Union Canal. This is an expensive trip and involves fundraising. Through this I get to know more people in the village and so perhaps I help to expand the community involvement of our children.

174

'Ricochet Counsell' is now my nickname because of the way I steered the boat up the canal, and especially through the Blisworth Tunnel. I seemed to tack, rebounding from one wall to the other all the way through! I do admit to being terrible at steering, but I did improve as the week went on!

The trip is a huge success. On the first morning of our trip the children all meet in the galley. They are sitting around the table with me waiting for their breakfast. I am sitting with them not saying a word. After a time one boy says, 'I want breakfast.'

'I want mine too,' I reply. It has taken about ten minutes for the boys to realize that they have to get the breakfast. What confusion and chaos there is as they look for the things they need for their breakfast, but what delight on the last morning – six days later – when we are all having cereal, bacon, egg, fried bread and tomatoes with toast and coffee, all served most acceptably and without any confusion, and cooked without a word of direction from any member of staff.

We have similar experiences with dressing. The boys are sitting on their bunks, at the beginning of the trip, waiting for the staff to decide for them what they are going to wear – that is what the majority of house parents do back at school. By the end of the week the children are dressing themselves in whatever they want to wear. To me this seems real progress and is really useful to the fourteen- to sixteen-year-olds on this trip.

My experience in the hospital service has taught me how easy it is for the handicapped person to be misunderstood and for his actions to be misinterpreted. Like the seventeen-year-old spastic patient I knew in my last hospital job. He had had a part-time job in a garage where he washed cars and cleaned up. He could manage bold hand movements very well, but his handicap did not allow him to make fine ones and he could not manage the zip on his trousers. After visiting the toilet one day at the garage he appeared on the forecourt seeking help with his trousers. His speech was very difficult to understand and he was reported for indecent exposure and sent to the subnormality

175

hospital under a court order which classified him as a sexual offender.

I would not like any of the children in my care to have habits which could lead to such unfortunate consequences. The school is isolated and since there is no need to draw curtains – for there is no public to see in through the windows – they are left open. But our children need to form ordinary social habits and I suggest that what they don't do in school they will not do out of school. Often nude bodies are to be seen at the dormitory windows at bedtime and in the mornings; if this were to happen in a town or in a normal community it could be classed as indecent exposure. Our children are innocent enough but they are not aware of the consequences of their actions and I suggest that while they are in school we should be helping them to form socially acceptable habits. Past experience has taught me that little things like drawing the curtains are, rightly or wrongly, important to the general social integration of the handicapped.

The care staff do a magnificent job and are always so busy but the children are a handful and often there are too few members of staff to do the job properly.

There are similar problems with the use of the toilet. The boys don't use the urinals and they perform with the toilet door open, so when they are out of school they have no idea of how to use a public convenience in the usual manner and consequently attract attention to themselves. Some of them cannot adjust their clothing and will ask anyone at hand to help them. I think, however, that their clothing should be adapted so that they can manage it by themselves. What is acceptable in the school is often going to be unacceptable in the outside world.

The school has a small swimming pool which the staff are allowed to use with their families after school. I enjoy taking my own children swimming but try as I might, I still cannot swim and encounter the same old problem with my hips. The pool is not very deep, about three feet six inches, and the water is always warm.

It is encouraging to see changes in school policy. The

176

principal has decreed that the school urinals must be used by every boy who possibly can, that their clothing will be adapted so that they can manage it themselves, and that curtains will be drawn by the children whenever they dress or undress.

Home life continues to be the most pleasing and stabilizing part of my life. My marriage, my independence and the affection of my family make all my past struggles worthwhile. Whenever I enter my home I can feel an almost physical release of pressure. I am accepted for what I am; here I have no need to prove myself and there is no competition. There is acceptance, peace and harmony, which are a therapy and make it possible for me to work and face the world.

Grant is now five and is attending the village school. He has been going to the local playgroup and knows many of the children who are with him at school. I am not happy about him starting school and I am surprised at this. It is as though I don't want Grant to be influenced by anyone other than his mother and me. I am sure I will get used to these outside influences as he settles down, but the feeling is strong. I was not aware of it until the time came for Grant to go to school – it is amazing how little we know of ourselves!

My son seems to be a bit deaf. The family doctor is making an appointment for us to see a specialist at the hospital. The specialist has discovered that the problem with Grant's hearing is small and is going to perform a minor operation to remove some fluid which has collected behind the ear, and to take his adenoids out. He will only be in hospital one day but the prospect worries me. Kathleen and I have been told that there is a six-month waiting list but I cannot sit around waiting for my son to be seen to. I ring the hospital regularly to inquire where Grant's name is on the waiting list. I know I am being a nuisance but within two months we are offered a bed; someone who should have gone into hospital has developed a cold and cannot be operated on, so the hospital has sent for Grant.

Kathleen has always brought Grant to hospital for his appointments while I have been at work, but today I feel I should be there to support her while Grant undergoes surgery. I wish I could go through this ordeal for him. I am left alone with Grant for a while and, for no reason that I can see, a nurse is putting cot sides at Grant's bed. This disturbs him. I imagine that he feels like a caged animal and is wondering what will happen next. I am asking very politely if they can be removed. I did not expect such a reaction from the young nurse: she has not said a word but has run down the ward and is bringing the sister to me.

Grant is crying uncontrollably now as I try to comfort him through the bars and sister is trying to assert her authority. 'I don't know who you are but you are upsetting my patient and my nurses. I see no need for you to be rude to my staff, so would you leave the ward?' After all these years such situations still keep arising.

'Sister, my son is disturbed by the bars around his bed. All I asked was were they necessary?'

I am rescued from the situation by the return of my wife who comes to my side and helps me to comfort Grant. She looks quizzically at sister and me.

'He is upset by the bars,' I say.

Sister has drawn herself to her full stature and inquires of my wife, 'Is *this* your husband?'

'Yes. Why?' answers Kathleen.

Sister is retreating down the ward and I am left to explain what happened.

I feel depressed that Grant should have witnessed this incident, but unfortunately he will have to come to terms with such things – they seem to be part of my life. However, the operation has been a success and Grant is now able to hear properly.

I am enjoying my work more and more and becoming involved in areas of the school's activity which are new to me. I cooperate with the school psychologist, which I find interesting. But when I was filmed on video, I was shocked to see myself on the screen. I had no idea that my handicap was still so noticeable. Each movement I make betrays my state. I had thought I could almost pass as normal if I were merely walking. But now, as I look at myself, each time I move my

178

hands I am amazed at my posture and appearance. It is absolutely no use becoming depressed about this: I am the same now as I was before I saw myself on film and I am never going to be able to hide what I am.

The principal would like to offer me promotion but my qualifications, which all appertain to the health service, are not recognized by the Department of Education and Science and so he cannot. I am advised to apply for a state teacher-training course so that I might get a Certificate of Education. But my efforts are futile, and filling in application form after application form from different colleges is incredibly frustrating. I did, in desperation, send off an application form to one college without mentioning my handicap, but I was still unsuccessful. Almost all of my applications that give precise details of my physical condition have not received a reply. In spite of this I enjoy life. My daughter is now four and my son seven. Kathleen is expecting our third child and we are again thrilled. The lovely midwife who attended Kathleen when Marcia was born has retired and we feel disappointed, because it was relaxed having Marcia's birth in our home, but we can see the wisdom of a hospital confinement.

Having visited the hospital for antenatal care my wife has got to know a little about the place where our baby will be born. I can be with Kathleen during the labour and at the birth and we both feel reassured by this. When my wife eventually goes into labour and is admitted into hospital, there is a misunderstanding with the midwife who has been assigned to us and whom we have never met before. She thinks she knows better than my wife when the baby is about to be born. I cannot stand to see my wife distressed as well as uncomfortable and I am afraid that the tension of the situation leads me to be rather rude. After all, my wife has had two babies previously and should know when her third one is about to appear – despite the midwife's theory that it will not be born for hours. After a frantic dash to the delivery room, the baby is born; mother and daughter are transferred to the aftercare ward.

The sister on this ward is Indian and has stopped me on my

179

way out. 'Mr Counsell, may I have a word with you?' She
invites me into her office by gesture of her hand. 'Sit down,
please. Have you had some trouble or has something upset
you today?'

I express my disapproval of my wife's treatment during
her labour and ask how she knew that I had been troubled.

'The nurse who brought your wife from the delivery room
was told to tell us that you were a troublemaker but when she
made her report, the doctor was with me and she happens to
know you. She is the paediatrician from the school where
you work. The doctor said it was out of character for you to
make trouble so I thought I would have a word with you.'

I find this sister down-to-earth and easy to talk with and as
the story unfolds I am surprised to hear her saying that she
will inquire about my complaint and that I must see her on
my next visit to the hospital.

Visiting time is over all too quickly and I hate to be parted
from my wife and new daughter for twenty-four hours. Sister
is waiting for me once again as I leave the ward.

'I did have a word with the midwife who delivered your
wife and you have every right to complain. The trouble is
that the midwife is very young and she thought that because
of your handicap you wouldn't know what labour was all
about. She also thought that there must be something wrong
with your wife if she was married to you. You must be very
used to this kind of thing happening in your life. I am Indian
and similar things happen to me.'

It seems that most minority groups suffer from the
ignorance and fear shown by other people that I sometimes
experience. It is a pity that most people react to what they
see, rather than to potential or facts. But then, people react
to tradition, and many minority groups are damned because
of tradition, be they dark-skinned or spastic. In days gone
by, handicapped people often were labelled as 'village idiots'
and foreign people, particularly blacks, were outcasts in our
society. Such traditions must die out before we see an end to
some of the fears and ignorance which surround minority
groups. I can hardly believe that my wife suffered at the
hands of the midwife just because I have a handicap. There is

absolutely nothing wrong with my wife, and yet the midwife treated her as an imbecile just because she has a handicapped husband. These kind of incidents have happened all through my life, but talking to the Indian sister has made me realize that there are a great many kinds of handicap, some not recognized as such.

The daughter my wife has just given birth to is a delightful baby, we have named her Emma Kate and she has already brought us a great deal of happiness.

9

Now I am the father of three children. I would never have thought my adult life could be this happy. I have been handicapped all my life and although I think that I now integrate and work well with normal people, there is always a strain; I am conscious of a barrier – sometimes only a slight barrier – when I am with normal people. That barrier disappears when I am with my wife: then there is no self-consciousness, I am completely relaxed, and this makes me a different person when I am at home.

I am still applying for places at teacher-training colleges, but up to now I have not been accepted.

Having returned to work after the summer holidays this morning, I am immediately summoned to the principal's office, where the deputy principal is waiting for me.

The principal has been taken to hospital with heart trouble and is unable to return to work for a long period. I am being asked if I will be an acting head of house while the principal is away. As head of house I am responsible for the day-to-day running of a unit with thirty children. I am awed at the opportunity but welcome the challenge. It is a great responsibility and I am grateful for the confidence which the principal and deputy principal have shown in me in offering me such a chance.

While the principal is away I undertake many of his public commitments and travel around the area speaking to various groups about the work of the school. I enjoy all of this, and the travelling and socializing I enjoy enormously. I remember telling someone on one of these visits about my difficulties in trying to get a place in teacher-training college.

Very late this evening, after my wife and I have gone to bed, I receive a telephone call from a person whom I do not know asking me if I would be willing to apply for a place at Homerton College in Cambridge. I thought that this was a teacher-training college for women, but my caller is telling me that it now takes male students as well.

Of course I apply, not thinking much of my chances but I am called for an interview. It is a rather unusual one, because the people who are interviewing me sound as though they really want to help, and as though they are willing to have me on their course. But it is a postgraduate course and as I am not a graduate, they must get permission from some higher authority. I have to write a letter listing all my employment experience, giving details of all my qualifications and saying why I want to do teacher training. This letter, along with a reference from the principal of the school, is sent to the college and after waiting a short time I receive an offer of a place with the postgraduate course.

I am wild with excitement and so are my wife and the principal. I am lucky enough to receive a grant from the county council and unpaid secondment from my work. This means my job will be waiting for me when I have completed my college course. Not only that, but the principal, who has returned to work although he is still quite ill, has given me a letter of appointment which, when I successfully complete my teacher training, will enable me to return as head of house. This is tremendously good news and means that my salary will then be substantially greater than at present.

All through my life I have been helped to acquire self-confidence by the people around me. Fundamentally, though, I am not a confident person, particularly when I have to meet strange people in a new situation. I may appear assured – even aggressive – and seem to have an outgoing personality, but this is a façade; I put great effort into concealing my feelings of inadequacy. I am never sure how strangers are going to respond to me and so I start my year at Homerton with the usual trepidation.

One of the handymen at Meldreth Manor School has been teaching me to swim and has actually managed to get me swimming on my back. I cannot do a recognizable back-stroke but I can now swim in my own way. I intend to go on practising and see if I can make progress. It has taken me forty years to get this far.

My college course is not like any of my previous courses. It is far more academic and the students are all postgraduates, far more used to scholarship of this kind than I am. Even my first day is difficult, as my dreadfully slow handwriting prevents me from taking down all the notes I should. We have discussion groups and I find it difficult to contribute because of the sophisticated language the other students use and the speed of the discussion. At lunchtime we are invited to have drinks with the college principal. I find this sort of occasion quite difficult. If I have a glass in my hand I really have to concentrate so as not to spill the contents, but here I am expected to make conversation as well as manage my glass. I want to make a good impression, it being my first day here, but I have managed to throw my drink down both myself and the tutor who is talking to me. It is not a question of spilling it, my hand jerks involuntarily and the contents of the glass slurp out. I wonder what kind of an idiot I look in the eyes of others as I spend the rest of the day in my drink-stained clothes.

My wife and family are still active in the Mormon Church but suddenly, after all these years, I am beginning to question whether it is right for me. I think the reason for this lies in a book which I have been reading, Thomas McPherson's *Philosophy and Religious Belief*. The book gives an account of many religions, including various forms of Christianity, and the philosophical thinking behind them. In reading it, and in looking at my religion in an objective way, I have become more aware of my own need for a sense of intellectual creativity, and I am unhappy with my thinking and feelings. I have studied a book called *The Education of the Brain Damaged Child*, by W. A. Cruikshank which gives information about the functions of the various parts of the brain, and I have discovered that the part of my brain which controls the emotions may well be damaged; as my religious

184

beliefs have an appeal to my emotions I wonder if my judgement could have been wrong. It is difficult to define spiritual and emotional feelings, but I am confused by religion. I find it difficult as well to alter my life style, as I have been a practising Mormon for twenty years. My conscience does not tell me anything, but then I am not doing anything against my conscience. I am merely having a fresh look at my beliefs and their origins and seeking to do that which is right.

I have thought about my marriage too, for if my emotional mechanisms are damaged then I wonder if my choice of wife was the right one. But this is ridiculous, as Kathleen and I have been so happy together. It is just religion that worries me, although, of course, our religion has been part of our marriage; I must remember that Kathleen accepted me as her husband knowing that I was of the Mormon faith, and our marriage has been in keeping with the doctrines of the Church. Now I want to change all that, but I must consider how my wife and family will react. My doubts as to the credibility of the Church are causing me to feel that I have deceived my wife and myself all these years. I do not think that this matter will be settled overnight; I need time to work it out.

The standard of work which the other students produce seems far superior to mine, but they have had years of academic training while I have not. Nevertheless, I do have practical experience to offer; this is my contribution to the course and I seem to integrate well with my fellow students.

I have had lectures in college recently about how to teach religion in school, one or two of which were vaguely connected with a humanitarian philosophy; I am not sure whether these have stimulated my thoughts or whether the fact that I have been thinking deeply about personal issues has something to do with age or maturity. I seem to be thinking more deeply than ever before. I wonder if I joined the Mormon Church for the right reasons? At that time in my life I needed companionship and active participation in something. Certainly the Church helped me to overcome many problems and filled a social void. I did a lot of public speaking for the Church, which helped my confidence greatly, and the Church leaders recognized my capabilities and gave me responsibility. This helped my self-respect; looking back, the fact that I was given these positions had nothing to do with my handicap, they were given to me because of my ability. Now my life seems shallow and I feel that perhaps I have been using or hiding behind the Church all these years, too scared to get involved in aspects of life unconnected with the Church. There are many areas in the community where I might be useful and where I would like to be involved, but I always use my Church commitments as an excuse not to. Maybe the truth of the matter is that I am scared of deeper integration. I am forced to look at myself and at my interaction with others. I am already looking at the way others react to me, perhaps too much so. The Church has been valuable to me but maybe I have used it as a prop, which I am now ready to dispense with.

There is one aspect of Church activity in which I have never been involved. All Mormons are supposed to be missionaries and spread the message wherever they are. I never could. I feel that because of my handicap I appear an oddity and being a Mormon makes me odder still. I have been sensitive about my religion and certainly my reluctance to engage myself in missionary work, both now and in the past, may indicate that I have never had a really deep conviction about the Church.

Fortunately I can still be a member without actively participating and I can take time to sort out my feelings without prejudice to my membership.

Many weeks have passed and many questions have I asked myself. I have come to a few conclusions. It is time I stopped using my handicap as an excuse to contract out of human relationships, if indeed that is what I have done. I should stop blaming my handicap for my problems. For example, my present feelings towards the Church seem to be a result of a natural process of maturing and yet I am still ready to find an excuse for my new thinking in my brain damage. There is also quite an element of 'look what I can do in spite of being handicapped' in my attitude to other people. I start to take special notice of how I respond to others and how differently I respond to each individual. I find I am relating to each one's personality and nothing else. I, too, must have a personality and people must respond to it. Ultimately, they do not respond only to my affliction. They may do initially but eventually they respond to my whole person. People are not really all that interested in my achievements, they don't respond to those. They respond to me, to my character. I feel a complete idiot. How could I have lived all this time without really thinking about this?

With a new philosophy I started a teaching practice this morning in a normal school. I do not know anyone at the school but I am certainly not going to discuss my handicap. It is obvious to everyone I meet. I am not even going to mention any problem which I think I may encounter while on this teaching practice. I am not going to speak about myself at all. I suppose, in a rather painful way, this all means that I have started to think of myself as normal and want to be judged as such, with no special concessions made for my handicap. In a way I have used and even almost bragged about my condition as a way to clamber up towards a normal life with normal social and professional interaction.

My first day has gone really well and the secret of this is that I have spent the entire day fighting off self-consciousness and in being interested in other people and in listening to them. I feel really pleased about today and feel confident that I am going to enjoy this teaching practice. I do not ever remember going into a new situation without mentioning some aspect of my handicap.

The children actually seem to be disappointed now that my teaching practice is at an end. My reports are good – I don't think I have ever done anything so well in my life. I have only mentioned my handicap when someone has asked a question about it, and I have never used it as an excuse, especially not to myself.

I have learned more about human relationships during this year than at any other time in my life. Previously I had been far too busy worrying about whether people were going to accept me despite my handicap and never realized just how much people wanted me to notice *them* and their achievements. I really was too selfish and inward-looking before.

While I am away at college the principal of Meldreth Manor has had to retire because of his health. My future at the school is now uncertain as the new principal does not want me back in the school in any other role than that of probationary teacher. This would mean a lower salary than I had expected on my return and a loss of status. A teacher direct from college going to work in a state school would need to do a probationary year, but Meldreth Manor School is privately owned and I have worked there for the past seven years; I also have a letter of appointment to return as a senior teacher. I turn for help to the National Union of Teachers and they advise and support me and do all they can to help. The crunch will come when I return to work, for the union cannot take any action until I am actually demoted or given a letter to that effect. As we live in a house that is tied to the job there is more than just my work at stake.

It would be better if I were to find a new position and I have already begun to apply for some. I manage to get a few interviews and have three posts offered to me. The one I choose to accept is at the Oliver Wells School in Milton Keynes. The school is to be a community and resource centre and integration of the handicapped will be one of its prime concerns, so it sounds interesting. Also, the former deputy principal at Meldreth, Trevor Jeavons, has been appointed headmaster at the Oliver Wells School and I like the idea of working with someone who knows my educational ideas and who is used to my way of teaching. I will have to do a probationary year because it is a state school. It is due to open in September 1978 so when I finish college at the beginning of July I can take a long summer holiday and settle into my new home in Milton Keynes. I am relieved that I do not need to return to Meldreth and I am looking forward to the future with confidence.

Looking back over the last eight years at Meldreth it has generally been a happy time. We loved the time spent there and towards the end of our stay we were all very involved

188

with village life. The children have grown up there and have lots of friends. Kathleen has run the village girl guides for the last five years, and it is with some regret that we leave.

Here we are now living in the city of Milton Keynes after my college assessments. I am now the proud owner of a Certificate of Education. We are living on one of the new housing estates in a development corporation house. The differences between life on this estate and life in Meldreth village is extreme. We don't like some aspects of life on the estate, so soon we have managed to buy a house in Bletchley and are settling down properly. Grant and Marcia, who now have to go to separate schools, are finding it a little hard to adjust to town life after the village, but eventually the local amenities win the day; there are far more things for them to do here. They soon make new friends and settle quite happily. Emma, our youngest, is now old enough to go to a playgroup and she soon makes friends too.

I am perfectly happy at my new school and consider that the new principal at Meldreth did me a good turn in driving me to leave his school; life is much more real here, not so isolated or protected. I have become involved in many committees and organizations. I am the chairman of the Milton Keynes Spastic Group, vice-chairman of a working party looking at statutory provision in the area, and a member of a committee looking at employment for the handicapped. I am an official visitor to a local children's home and have a wider interest in other people than I had before. I attend the Mormon Church from time to time, but I am still confused by religion.

Oliver Wells School is a special school catering for children with all types of handicaps and problems. I have a pleasant relationship with the rest of the staff and with the parents of the children as well. I no longer find it necessary, as I did at Meldreth, to justify my presence in the school to parents and find that I am far more relaxed with them; as I expect them to accept me, I don't think they notice my handicap very much.

I have discovered that the tables have turned. I have been helped in so many ways by so many people to cope with

189

my handicap but now I am using my handicap to help others.

The promotion which I was promised on my appointment to the school has been given to me now that I have completed my probationary year. I have an extra responsibility – an involvement with school leavers – which brings me into contact with more people in the community; I have been photographed for the newspaper and my views quoted. I feel I am becoming one of the local characters. I am a little bit afraid of this attention, as some reporters occasionally change what I have said or give my words a different meaning. Several times I have been recognized by people I do not know who have seen my photograph in the papers and at times I have felt almost like a celebrity.

The children in my first class at the Oliver Wells School have various handicaps. One boy of fourteen is not expected to live through this term; he has no idea that he is going to die. I find his plight distressing but I have to come to terms with it and treat the boy as normal. One fourteen-year-old girl, who has been injured in a road accident, must learn to be more independent and ask for help when she needs it rather than wait for it to be offered. One day I took my class out to a coffee bar to help them learn about ordinary behaviour in a public place. The traffic-accident girl just stood at the counter not knowing what to do. She is not able to carry her own cup and saucer because of her clumsy walk and shaky hands. She took it for granted that someone would help her but I hoped she would find the courage and the confidence to ask for assistance. Although she was very cross with me I made her ask one of the women behind the counter to help her, because that is what she would need to do were she on her own.

Quite a few of the children at the Oliver Wells School have a short life expectancy and quite a few more can expect a poor quality of life in adulthood because of the severity of their handicaps. For myself, I find it totally unrealistic to concentrate on teaching reading and writing to these latter pupils when they find these skills difficult anyway because of other problems. I would be the first to advocate formal

190

teaching for anyone with the necessary mental ability, without regard to physical handicap, but I feel that education should prepare one for life – and with some children that means developing an awareness of environment and of social acceptability. In retrospect, I myself learned more from my experiences after I left school than I did in school. I feel sure that many of the children at the Oliver Wells School too benefit more from social experiences and expeditions where they acquire knowledge in a relaxed way, than from spending their time in a classroom, tense, trying to do formal work and feeling like failures. I ask myself many times when I am in a formal situation with this type of child, am I playing at school?

All the children in my class have experienced failure at some stage and this has left most of them with severe insecurities, so much so that they have only a limited interest in reading and writing. I have to find devious ways to get them to participate in learning activities. I have involved them in a project which has got their interest: we are organizing a dinner for the staff and their partners at half-term and involving the children in this. They do not see the costing of items connected with the dinner as maths; nor do they see the writing of invitations as English. They are not aware that they are engaged in educational activities as they draw plans for seating arrangements and write out instructions for games we might play; nor do they suspect that measuring the room to see how many tables we can fit in is anything but a practical task. As the children prepare and cook the food and serve it they are delighted with themselves, but unaware that they have begun their academic education.

As with the majority of establishments which cater for the handicapped, the general public create a mystery about the place. It is largely a friendly mystique, but the old stigma, the attitudes of fear and estrangement toward the handicapped, lingers on. As we are a community centre and are involved with integration, it seems a good idea to invite other schools and groups in the area into the school to perform in an evening of Christmas music. The Oliver Wells children

191

are taking part as well and it is a smashing evening. We need a leader for the carol singing and I seem to be the only one willing to do it! I cannot conduct without a baton and as we don't have one, I have to use a paintbrush wrapped in tin foil, which serves the purpose well until bits of foil drop off while I am leading the singing! My colleagues think it is funny, but I feel a bit of an idiot!

We plan a canal trip in 1979 and again the children are involved in the preparation. Maths is much more meaningful when it has a purpose and whilst the children are a bit overawed by the calculations required, they enjoy doing them. It will be a test to see if these calculations prove correct when we are on the trip. The number of letters which are required in preparation for the expedition amount to a term's English topic and the children's delight when they receive replies to their letters is heartening.

To these children, history, geography and science might seem to be irrelevant if taught on their own, but when taught in connection with the canal trip they become meaningful and interesting. This trip is organized quite differently from previous ones I have been involved in, because the children are much more mentally able than the children at Meldreth. Two of the boys are supposed to be virtually unable to read, but they are the official engineers of our party. One of the boats has a mechanical defect and the boys are given the manual to find out how to repair it. They are so enthusiastic that they are not aware that they are understanding the printed word, and with very little assistance from the staff they are able to correct the fault. When questioned upon how they did it they both realize that they have read and understood the instructions. Their confidence soars and they are now more willing to cooperate in learning reading skills. Our other boat develops a major fault and we have to send for the shipping company's engineer. Naturally, as leader of the party I meet the man to tell him of our difficulties, but the man demands to see the person in charge.

'I am the person in charge,' say I, but the man demands to see someone responsible. He looks around the boats for another member of staff and whatever he says is relayed to me by the other teacher. Many of the children are watching all this and are gratifyingly indignant that this man ignores me. The discussion which follows is very enlightening and I suggest that the staff are learning more about the children from this talk than from any other source. The children want to know why I let him get away with his bad manners. I ask two questions in reply. Did the breakdown get repaired? Did I cause any unpleasantness when there was no need? The children have complained of similar treatment in their lives and I hope that by acting without hasty emotion I have taught them a lesson.

We have had a number of other school expeditions. One of these is an educational cruise. The party consists of ten children and four members of staff. We have with us a very bright fifteen-year-old girl whose physical handicap is quite obvious. People speak to her like they would to a pet dog, and she feels miserable about this. We are sitting on deck together surrounded by the rest of the group when a woman speaks to the girl in a very patronizing way. The girl responds by shrugging her shoulders. I remain with her after all the group have gone below, trying to explain how I think she should respond to such a situation.

As I do so, someone else stops to speak to us in a condescending way. I ignore what the woman is saying and comment on her coat. 'That is a very nice coat. It is real fur, isn't it?'

'Yes, it is. It is mink.'

'My friend here is hoping to design clothes when she leaves school.'

A conversation then develops between the woman and the girl which is spontaneous and natural, and I know the girl is learning something from this. Now whenever she is patronized she shows her intelligence by some comment or other instead of being flattered, and is developing more confidence.

How we came to be on this cruise is another story. Mark, a boy who had a very short time to live, was very difficult to motivate and I had to find a way of interesting him in something. I could not allow him just to sit in my classroom

193

until he died, although he was not aware that he was going to die. I asked his class one day during our first term what they would like to do if they knew the world was going to end next week. Mark spoke up and said that he had been on an aeroplane and every other mode of transport but he had never sailed on the seas. He went on to say how much he would like to go on a cruise. So Mark and I got to work on the possibility of a school cruise; we studied brochures, wrote letters, looked at maps and worked out what it would cost and how we could raise the money. I am sure that the stimulation which Mark received from this venture kept him alive longer than was expected.

Mark died three months after he returned from the cruise, but his parents tell me his time at the Oliver Wells was a happy one.

The improvement in Mark's personality and alertness while he was with us has had an effect on the people who knew him. The stimulation he gained in preparing the cruise as well as on the trip itself has encouraged interest in future expeditions. Many people have offered to help us financially this year but there are two fundraising events which moved me emotionally and which I feel I must mention.

Kevin Evans is a young man who lives in Milton Keynes who tried to beat the world record for pole squatting. The record is thirty days. This eighteen-year-old was sponsored to live in a barrel on top of a twenty-five foot pole to raise money for us to go on future cruises. I really admired his efforts but I was also aware of the other people – his promoters, his family etc. – who supported him. It makes me feel that others can see the good in our work and I am encouraged to go on.

The pole squat was a big attraction and brought a lot of attention both to Kevin and to the school, as well as £900. But I was not prepared for the scheme that Mark's parents launched after their boy had died. They wanted to try and beat the world record for a tower of ten-pence coins. This project was undertaken in Milton Keynes city centre and the tower was manned twenty-four hours a day for two whole weeks. And either Mark's dad or mum could be found there

194

no matter what time of day or night one visited the tower. Over £2000 was raised.

After three years at the Oliver Wells I now have quite a senior position and am involved with all the age groups throughout the school in training for self-sufficiency, independence and improvement of self-image. My work includes extensive work with those soon to leave school and go out into the world, and I also have a responsibility to foster community relations, so that the school may develop as a community project helping the pupils to integrate. I have a very unusual job description, which has evolved as my head teacher has seen the results of my work. It is only realistic to say that my own experience of life has equipped me for my job. My handicap has been my teacher and I feel that perhaps through the hand of fate I have arrived at a point in my life where I can make purposeful use of my handicap to try and help others.

1981, the International Year of the Disabled, was a hectic year for me. I don't think a week went by without addressing one group or another. I spoke to groups about the Spastics Society in Milton Keynes, about the Oliver Wells School, about my life. But the highlight of the year was being invited to Homerton College, in Cambridge, to speak to about 100 students and tutors about my views on the integration of handicapped people into the community. When I compare my lack of communication in my early years with occasions like this I am astonished. It is a thrill for me to stand before an audience knowing that they understand what I am saying and to have this knowledge confirmed by the questions I receive at the end of my speech. I am not unique in my achievements: many have achieved more than I against worse odds, but my optimism has lead me in the paths of ability and accomplishment I once could not have dreamt of.

10

From time to time I return to Blackburn to visit my family and friends. The place had already begun to change before I left eleven years ago. After my father's retirement the bakehouse was sold and became a betting shop. I viewed this with nostalgia, remembering the part that the old building had played in my earlier life. But now the whole town, particularly the Audley district, has changed. Alker Street has been destroyed. The family home is gone. So is the bakehouse, the doctor's surgery and grandmother's home. My childhood world has taken on a new shape through redevelopment. The cobbled streets where I used to play have been replaced by modern road surfaces and in place of the old terraced houses there are modern homes. The atmosphere has changed, but one or two buildings still remain to remind me that my childhood was not a dream. The church on Audley Range with its steep spire and railing which I used to try to climb, the school where I was taught and the mill where I began my working life are still there. I can scarcely recognize the child who played and struggled there. Change is all around us, for not only do towns change with redevelopment but attitudes change as well.

In my work I can compare my childhood and upbringing with that of handicapped children today. I have no regrets, nor am I critical of modern ways and treatments. In this modern world, however, it seems to me that there are not enough Mammy Earnshaws, Mammy Brogdens or Mammy Bucks. And while there may be many grandmothers like mine, there are too few extended families, and all too many that are scattered across the country, with young parents living away from the grandparents. What marvellous support my parents had from neighbours and family, and what valuable lessons I learned from that support.

The other week I took four children to a leisure complex in Milton Keynes to collect a sum of money which had been raised by the man in the barrel to help to finance a school cruise. We had to wait a considerable time in the manager's office for a press photographer. The people in the office were kind and chatty and offered our pupils tea or coffee, chips, chocolate or anything from the snack bar below. These offers were met with grunts, not even a 'thank you' was heard from any of our four young people. Not one of them had a word to contribute to the conversation that was aimed at them while they sat waiting in the office. They sat, almost masochistically making themselves appear more handicapped than they really are. After observing these four students I am concerned that they be given experiences which will help them overcome their problems. I suggest that this is a priority in their education. All these people are over the age of fifteen and it is painful for me to watch them. I know how they feel. It is something more than shyness, more than a lack of social skill, it is something more than being scared of people. Their parents are often unaware of this social handicap in their offspring but they can help their children in many ways. It is often through involvement in out-of-school activities that we can counsel the parents on such issues.

I recognize myself at a younger age as I look at these young people. I was fifteen when I started work and I did not know how to respond to people; nor was I aware of how my lack of response made me appear and how it caused embarrassment and created an atmosphere. It was my life at the mill and, in particular, Raymond and Arthur, who taught me to see the problem and who helped me to overcome it. They gave me actual examples of the words I could use to reply to others and they told me how stupid I looked when I did not reply. It's interesting now to reflect that Raymond and Arthur (neither of them well educated or sophisticated), befriended, involved and treated me with enormous sensible intelligence

197

as well as kindness. I owe them more than I realized at the time.

It took many years before my responses to people were spontaneous and reflected my actual thinking. It is not until one has a spontaneous, unreserved contribution to make to a gathering that one is able to integrate. By this, I mean a physical as well as a verbal contribution.

The concerns of some of our school leavers of seventeen and eighteen years of age certainly reflect a lack of confidence, a lack of experience and an unease in forming relationships with strangers, whether they be fleeting or longlasting.

'How do I get married?' asks a seventeen-year-old boy.

'I don't know how to talk to people. I don't know how to make friends.'

I do not have the answers to these questions. But each time they are raised I feel fortunate to have had friends, parents, family and experiences that have helped me to overcome the same problems. I am aware that as I learned, when I was younger, from experiences and from practising newly learned social skills, my self-image changed. As this improved I was able to work out the answers to such questions for myself. I try to give the children at school experiences which will improve their self-respect and self-image, and hope that these situations will bring answers to their questions. A few children have made such good progress while they have been with us that they have been placed in mainstream education. They do not have bad physical problems but tend to have learning difficulties which we have helped them to overcome to an extent. Our children have found it difficult to mix with the children of the mainstream schools. They have been threatened, cajoled, persuaded, pushed. We have used every possible means to help them integrate and they simply cannot do it. They are frightened and have no idea of how to make relationships. I hope to do a study on the reasons why some children – not only handicapped ones – are unable to interact socially with others. I do not know whether teaching or structured remedial programmes are sufficient to help these children, but I hope that they might meet in their lives

198

the kind of people I met in mine and that they might have experiences which will help them to emerge from isolation.

My own children often have friends to stay and I have noticed how they learn to be accepted while accepting the other children. They have the opportunity to try out their thoughts and express these thoughts to others. They also eventually become aware of other people's lives and make comparisons. The questions which my children have asked of my wife and me at each stage of their development reflect their concern for and growing ability in forming relationships. This is particularly interesting to me because the more I watch my children develop, the more I become aware of my own childhood isolation and its effects.

As I look back to the beginning of my working life I realize that I had to learn to think in terms of speech. As a child I had learned to think but did so without expressing my thoughts to others, and there is a vast difference in the thinking which I had developed and the thinking needed in using speech. There was a long period when it took concentrated effort for me to formulate replies to comments and conversation. Normally, the learning of language is incidental, and one's involvement in conversation becomes spontaneous in as much as one is not aware of thinking about the words used. I am still very much aware of the words I use, of the mistakes I make in pronunciation, and concerned about the way I form the sounds to make my words, for I wish to speak with clarity. I am still learning.

Although I have overcome many of my problems, I am still handicapped. I find fulfilment in living a full and ordinary life but I still need help and support. I have not got the confidence to send out a letter from the school without the headmaster at my school reading it before it is typed: I am aware of my stilted and limited ability to express myself in writing.

There are still those who may laugh at me and misunderstand me, for in many situations I look peculiar. But this is only because they make comparisons which label me as 'different'. If only I could be viewed as an individual. If only people would realize that I was born the way I am and that for me to talk and use my body the way I do is normal. Were I to speak or use my hands and body like the majority of people I would not be me. It is absolutely normal for me to function the way I do. If it were not for those comparisons maybe I might be seen as a person rather than as an oddity. But I remember how, as a child in my carry-cot, my family noticed how I responded to the trees above in the park, and so encouraged me to reach for my toys by suspending them above me. I remember how, however worried and baffled they were about me, they always showed me great loyalty and would never tolerate outside criticism. They forced me to understand the meanings of things, by demonstration and explanation, even though they thought then that I would never be able to speak for myself. I know that father told Olive, Joe and the others that I was an individual and not to be compared with others. They tell me that the first time I ever tried to communicate something other than my own needs – the day I tried to tell mother about the yeast horse outside the bakehouse, when I was six – the whole family understood the significance and were buoyant.

I hope that I will continue to make progress and enjoy life. These days, I may be unfashionable in being optimistic, but I suppose I have more reason than most to carry hope with me.